LIZ LOCHHEAD

Liz Lochhead is a poet, playwright and occasional theatre director. She was born in Lanarkshire in 1947 and educated at Glasgow School of Art. Her collections of poetry include *Dreaming Frankenstein*, *The Colour of Black & White* and *True Confessions*, a collection of monologues and theatre lyrics.

Her original stage plays include *Dracula*, *Mary Queen of Scots Got Her Head Chopped Off*, *Blood and Ice*, *Perfect Days* and its 'sister play' *Good Things*. Her many stage adaptations include Molière's *Tartuffe*, *Miseryguts* (based on *Le Misanthrope*) and *Educating Agnes* (based on *L'École des Femmes*); as well as versions of *Medea* by Euripides (for which she won the Scottish Book of the Year Award in 2001), and *Thebans* (adapted mainly from Sophocles' *Oedipus* and *Antigone*).

Liz lives in Glasgow. She became the city's Poet Laureate in 2005.

D1428019

Liz Lochhead

MARY
QUEEN OF SCOTS
GOT HER HEAD
CHOPPED OFF

NICK HERN BOOKS

London

www.nickhernbooks.co.uk

A Nick Hern Book

This revised version of *Mary Queen of Scots Got Her Head Chopped Off* first published in 2009 by Nick Hern Books Limited, 14 Larden Road, London W3 7ST

First published in an earlier version in 1989 by Penguin Books, London

Mary Queen of Scots Got Her Head Chopped Off copyright © 1987, 2009 Liz Lochhead

Introduction copyright © 2009 Liz Lochhead

Liz Lochhead has asserted her right to be identified as the author of this work

Cover image: Miniature of Mary Queen of Scots, c.1560 by François Clouet (c.1510-72) (follower of), Victoria & Albert Museum/The Bridgeman Art Library
Cover design: Ned Hoste, 2H

Typeset by Nick Hern Books, London
Printed in the UK by CPI Bookmarque, Croydon, Surrey

A CIP catalogue record for this book is available from the British Library

ISBN 978 1 84842 028 1

Mixed Sources
Product group from well-managed forests and other controlled sources
www.fsc.org   Cert no. TT-COC-002227
© 1996 Forest Stewardship Council
FSC

Introduction

In the autumn of 1984 I was in Portree on the Isle of Skye doing some poetry readings for pupils in the high school. After the bell went at four I was heading for the lonely B&B and my library book when I saw, in the butcher's window, a poster advertising Communicado Theatre Company's production of *Carmen, the Play.* Couldn't believe my luck. It was on tonight!

They were my pals too. Gerry Mulgrew had, earlier that year, played (brilliantly and all too convincingly) a talking dog in a musical touring piece I'd written for Wildcat Theatre Company called *Same Difference.* He served as both chorus and narrator, Toby Dug, complete with saxophone, talking, rapping, relating directly to us. The audience loved him, and so did I.

That spring, as we'd rehearsed, every tea break had found him reading Prosper Merimée's novel or deep in big historical tomes on the Spanish Civil War, because *his* Carmen, planned for his own burgeoning company, was to be set then, with the eponymous gypsy crossing back and forth across the lines, loyal only to her own survival and the flame of her passion for Don Jose, the Man in the Suit of Lights.

Now it was autumn and Communicado – having, that August, been the toast of the Edinburgh Festival Fringe and with sold-out weeks in the Donmar Warehouse in London and in the USA under their belts – were on tour all over Scotland. Here on Skye I easily tracked down the van outside the venue, found the company inside putting all the seats for the audience on the stage so they could play on the floor, helped them humph the minimal bits of set. And that night, as near 7.30 as was decent in the Highlands, the lights went down on one of the most thrilling pieces of theatre I've ever seen.

Two beautiful girls played the fiddle, conjuring the story out of the darkness, Alison Peebles blew the smoke from her cigarette through the slats of a Venetian blind and, with a pull of the cord and a lighting change, was revealed in a tilted beret and a raggy vintage bit of finery from a charity shop as just the sexiest, most amoral, most fascinating Carmen ever.

Stephen Jeffreys' terrific play, a radical retelling of an old story for his own purposes, remained a beacon for me later as I struggled with my version of the Mary Queen of Scots myth for Gerry and this groundbreaking company. To my enduring delight and pride it has become a Communicado – and national – landmark, joining *Carmen* and Edwin Morgan's wonderful rhyming Scots translation of Rostand's *Cyrano de Bergerac* and Mulgrew's own storytelling productions of the tinker-ish *Tall Tales for Long Dark Nights* and *Arabian Nights* and – only last month – *Tam O'Shanter*.

How I remember *Mary Queen of Scots Got Her Head Chopped Off* coming about was this: Gerry Mulgrew had the idea.

And, once his *Carmen* tour was done, he took me for a Chinese meal and said he wanted to do a Mary Queen of Scots Show and that he wanted me to write it. This must've been early in 1985, and already he was thinking forward to 1987, when it was going to be the four hundredth anniversary of Mary's decapitation at the hands of her cousin Elizabeth. With his producer's hat on, Mulgrew thought Communicado's Festival Fringe piece for that year ('If we can get the grant,' he said) ought to commemorate this. He felt that the very fact it was the anniversary of Mary's *death* rather than her birth we'd be remembering was perhaps the start of an interesting story already? 'It'll really sell, there'll be loads of attention for this subject, someone'll do that Schiller play,' I remember him saying. (The Official Festival did, indeed, with Hannah Gordon as Mary.)

It all seemed a long way ahead, more than two and a half years. I was delighted to say yes. It didn't, that night, matter that neither of us seemed to know much of anything of the history, except the blunt axe-man ending, and... oh, yes, we had both dim memories of a childhood game played by flicking the heads off dandelions while chanting 'Mary-Queen-of-Scots-Got-Her-Head-Chopped-Off, Mary-Queen-of-Scots-Got-Her-Head-

Chopped-Off...' We were, though, already very aware that, culturally, as a Scot of Irish-Catholic descent (Gerry) and I, of solidly Lowland Scottish Presbyterian stock, had been brought up with totally different versions of the myth. The Catholic Mary is certainly a martyr and almost a saint; the Proddy version of Mary veers between limp victim and politically inept nymphomaniac devil-woman who almost scuppered Our Glorious Reformation. Of course we had long put by such childish things. Naturally, we were each at war with our own cultural biases – for example: I was as much exercised by the misogyny of John Knox, his enduring anti-feminist, anti-feminine legacy in Scottish society, as Gerry was attracted by the notion that Knox's teaching the people to read so they could read the Bible for themselves and the Protestant ideal of a direct one-to-one relationship with God, un-mediated by any clerical hierarchy, had directly led to democracy. We were both republican and anti-royalist. So it might seem odd that we would soon be so wound up in the emotions of this long-ago royal tragedy. But anyway we made a deal, Gerry would apply for a commission from the Arts Council to pay me for a script, he would get on with the next Communicado Project and, together and separately, we'd start work on the Mary Queen of Scots Show for the Edinburgh Festival Fringe, August 1987 – and then to tour.

Flash forward to June 1987 and I'm up all night, unable to go to bed as the horror unfolds and the election results come in. For the third time Margaret Thatcher gets back in to power. We can't believe it. Nobody in Scotland can believe it. We voted resoundingly against the Tories in this country and yet we are being ruled by them. Again. That Friday there is a palpable sense of gloom everywhere, and at Glasgow Queen Street I actually consider getting on the wrong train, running away, instead of boarding the train to go to that meeting in Edinburgh in Communicado's wee borrowed office to tell Gerry that we don't have a play to go into rehearsal with next month. Yes, there are scenes and fragments all over the place, we both know there are those wee bits we like, that speech of the Corbie character with the pan-Scotland overview, that sexy scene between Leicester and Elizabeth, that plotting scene where Mary, imprisoned in that castle, gets that brewer to help her get messages out to her English Catholic allies, there is mibbe something in that cruel kids' stuff but it doesn't fit with anything else… I've got a trunk-load of research material (I had increasingly spent more and more hours that spring in Glasgow's Mitchell Library doing more and more 'research' – i.e. Not Writing the Play). 'Gerry, I've got all these scenes, but we don't have a play. We go into rehearsal next month and by then I'll have to have found you a do-able one among all the literally hundreds there are about her, the library catalogues say so. I'll start reading today. I can't write the Mary Queen of Scots play you wanted. And the bloody Tories are in again.'

Gerry is amazing. He refuses, just won't release me from the job of doing this piece. No, we've promised an original world premiere of a Mary Queen of Scots Show. It doesn't have to be a proper play. (He says this like it's the last thing he'd have wanted.) He says – as a way out of this impasse – to simply tell the story as a folk tale, and then Communicado can dramatise this folk tale, in the way they did *Arabian Nights*. He says to imagine how *King Lear* would be as a fairy story. *Once upon a time there was a King who had three daughters, and he decided to divide his kingdom between them, so he called them together and*… 'Just write once upon a time,' he says… 'What would that be? And we'll go from there.'

So that night, back home in Glasgow, I find myself writing down – just as part of a process, that was all he'd meant it to be – 'Once upon a time there were twa queens on the wan green island.' And then realising just how well that fitted Corbie's voice…

From that point, so late in the day, the piece came to life. For a team of eight already in place – not Communicado's style to necessarily have a play written before casting it – including both Alison Peebles and also Anne Wood, one of those wonderful fiddlers from *Carmen*, and a dancer no one knew yet that Gerry really wanted to work with and the amazing Myra McFadyen we all loved for whom the chorus/narrator/backbone-of-piece role had initially been conceived, and long tall Anne Lacey, with her flag of long pale red hair and face from a Flemish painting, to be Mary.

Burning midnight oil, as I did just about every night from then until we opened, I was never happier.

I can remember, just a week before rehearsals began, coming up with what seemed like a good solution for how to do the murder of Riccio for this tiny cast. (In reality, more than a dozen armed men broke in and murdered Mary's secretary before her very eyes as she sat with a few trusted servants in Holyrood Palace.) Oh, but I could do it as a play-within-a-play and it could be a horrid-comical masque of Salome, which would end up with a different head on a plate... It was, for me, from now on, just simply a matter of getting on with it, and the sheer enjoyment of the rhyming and the Stanley Holloway parodying, and taking down those most passionate speeches for Mary which seemed, whiles, to almost write themselves.

When we did go into rehearsal, about three quarters of what is now here was extant. Not necessarily in the right order – I don't like to admit it but the Bairns scene was the beginning of the play, not the end. And although the first half ended properly with the wedding of Mary and Darnley, there was the wrong rhythm and build-up in the earlier scenes, which were all about the different contemporaneous circumstances and forces ranged against the queens in both Scotland and England until Elizabeth sends Darnley north, and Mary falls for him, chooses him. Her first dramatic – and disastrous – *action*.

But, at the end of the first week, as the company struggled through a stagger-run of the first half, I saw quite clearly what the structure of the whole play should be. The Bairns were a coda, Corbie the beginning and – as Colin MacNeil the designer bravely, and so rightly, held off from making any irrevocable design decisions till he saw properly what the play *was* and came up with his perfect broken circus ring and fantastic anachronistic costumes, which were all, apart from terrific actors and performers, this play needs – I set about, more midnight oil, putting the shape of it to rights, as I had to, more Corbie-glue to write too, while poor Gerry, actually playing Knox as well as directing the piece and trying to see the whole arc of the thing, was understandably going crazy waiting for the script of everything from the Murder of Darnley till the death of Mary...

We got there in the end. With the play not yet *quite* in the shape that now goes into print, but definitely in the context of a debate about the then current state of affairs between Scotland and England that the play seemed to illuminate. Margaret Thatcher is not Queen Elizabeth the First, but questions of women and power – and how to hold on to it – are always there as we consider either icon. There was at that time a real sense of frustration in Scotland, a need for us to tell our own stories and find our own language to tell it in. Communicado had a bit of a mission about that, which I was proud to share.

It was a huge success. For Communicado – I honestly did not think any other theatre company would be able to do this play or would ever want to. And yet it has had quite a life. They study it in schools and universities. I've seen many other productions, professional and student and amateur, and enjoyed most of them very much. My friend David McVicar, now a world-famous opera director, did it at the Lyceum in Edinburgh with Daniela Nardini as Mary and also in upstate New York with a tiny little Puerto Rican powerhouse of an Elizabeth. He was tough with me about the gap he perceived in the published Penguin edition of the play, sure that I hadn't finished the 'historical' story satisfactorily nor bridged it properly into the anachronistic coda. In the nineties I wrote far too long a composite scene for David's production, resolving all the characters, and including a clumsier version of the simple scene in Mary's cell the night before the execution that I am pretty sure I have now, for the first time, got right.

I'll find out tomorrow. The National Theatre of Scotland go into rehearsal with this new production of my play in this version for their *Ensemble* strand. It'll be directed by the same Alison Peebles who played Elizabeth in the original production, and who was a founder member, back in 1983, of Communicado Theatre Company. We'll be looking at the model for the set and she'll be handing out scripts, pared and considered and finalised scripts with a beginning, a middle and a '*The End*'. There is a generous rehearsal schedule and proper resources. So it couldn't be more different from day one of rehearsals in the long since demolished filthy old tumbledown Lyceum Studio in 1987. In a few weeks from now there will be sixteen ninety-seater performances in small venues in mainly fairly remote areas of Scotland from Shetland to Dunoon, and, if it is a successful production, we are assured the National Theatre of Scotland will think again whether or not to give the production a further life in bigger venues in the major urban centres.

Which'll depend on the play finding a new context. Depend on there being a demand for it. When I look at it now it is clearly fundamentally about Mary and Elizabeth, the passion of these women to have sex and love and marriage – or not – for can they, without losing power? How do you have a full life as a woman and your full independence? All these things women are still struggling with. It's not as if these issues have been solved, or ever could be. It is, it seems to me, an eternal conflict. And so it remains a great story.

Communicado and Gerry Mulgrew still struggle from project to project trying to find funding for what they want to do, usually being turned down despite their past triumphs and their many long unpaid hours filling up forms and applications, such is the shockingly unfair and capricious distribution of resources for theatre in this country. Gerry's wild adaptation of *Tam O'Shanter* for Perth Theatre, which we saw just after Burns' Night this year showed a company, and a man, with creativity still in full flight.

Why I find myself, tonight, thinking back on the Communicado days and how *Mary Queen of Scots Got Her Head Chopped Off* began isn't nostalgia for the good-old-bad-old-days-when-we-had-nothing-and-everything, but a desire to get my own mojo back and working. I want to remind myself that nothing will come of nothing. Everything has its spark in previous creative endeavours, and it is these that give both the impetus and the context for the new.

It must've been Gerry recalling his daft role as that talking dog of mine that made him say, way back in 1985, initiating the whole project: 'Remember in the theatre you can do absolutely anything – we can have a talking crow, anything we want.' It was also, as luck would have it, that much of 1985 for me was spent working on translating Molière's *Tartuffe* into a new rhyming version which to my surprise came out in a Scots I didn't even know I had in me. A first foray into a language that was to evolve into a rather rich and strange (or so it seems to me now) Scots flowering for *Mary*, coming next. It was certainly seeing Communicado on Skye and falling in love with their whole rough-magic, storytelling, poor-theatre, total-theatre ethos that both made me desperate to do it, and also gave me the glimmerings of a writing style and even of a possible structure for the Mary Queen of Scots Show – which was as near a working title as the project ever had until the deadline for the poster copy. Gerry came into rehearsal and said: 'It's gone to print now and I just told the graphic designer it is called *Mary Queen of Scots Got Her Head Chopped Off*, it just suddenly came to me that was what it's called, OK?'

Apart from that title, I did, in the end, write and choose every word of the play. None of the dialogue or the scenes were improvised into being, though, God knows, the whole company tied themselves in knots trying all different ways of staging them and, especially, as is the Communicado trademark, segueing from one scene to the other. The 'Jock Tamson's Bairns' ending of *Mary,* though, did come out of an early workshop day about a year or more before rehearsals when – and I really can't remember whose initial idea this was – we considered: could we tell the whole story, do the whole play, as a set of contemporary children forced to re-enact a tragedy we didn't understand?

Liz Lochhead
22 February 2009

Mary Queen of Scots Got Her Head Chopped Off was first performed at the Lyceum Studio Theatre, Edinburgh, on 10 August 1987, with the following cast:

FIDDLER	Anne Wood
LA CORBIE	Myra McFadyen
MARY	Anne Lacey
ELIZABETH	Alison Peebles
HEPBURN O'BOTHWELL	Stuart Hepburn
KNOX	Gerard Mulgrew
DANCER / RICCIO	Frank McConnell
DARNLEY / LEICESTER	John Mitchell

Director	Gerard Mulgrew
Designer	Colin MacNeil

This revised version of the play was first performed at Druimfin, Tobermory, Mull, on 18 April 2009, in a production by the National Theatre of Scotland, which subsequently toured, with the following cast:

LA CORBIE	Joyce Falconer
MARY	Jo Freer
ELIZABETH	Angela Darcy
HEPBURN O'BOTHWELL	John Kielty
KNOX	Lewis Howden
RICCIO	Marc Brew
DARNLEY	Owen Whitelaw

Director	Alison Peebles
Designer	Kenny Miller
Lighting Designer	Lizzie Powell
Composer	David Paul Jones
Musical Director	John Kielty
Choreographer	Marc Brew

MARY QUEEN OF SCOTS
GOT HER HEAD CHOPPED OFF

Liz Lochhead

For Gerry Mulgrew,
without whom not a word of this play would have been written,
and for my colleagues in the Department of Scottish Literature
at the University of Glasgow from 2006 to 2009, who taught me
properly to value this as a text in its own right, rather than
only as a blueprint for future productions.

4

Characters

LA CORBIE
MARY/MARION/MAIRN/MAREE
ELIZABETH/BESSIE/LEEZIE/WEE BETTY
HEPBURN O'BOTHWELL
KNOX
RICCIO
DARNLEY

and others

Note

*Mary, when she speaks, has a unique voice. She's a
Frenchwoman speaking totally fluently, Braid Scots vocabulary
and all, in Scots, not English – but with a French accent.*

*Elizabeth has a robust, and almost parodic version of slightly
antique (think forties black-and-white films), very patrician RP.*

ACT ONE

Scene One

Scotland, Whit Like?

Music. An eldritch tune on an auld fiddle, wild and sad.

Alone, our chorus, LA CORBIE. An interesting, ragged, ambiguous creature in her cold spotlight.

CORBIE. Country: Scotland. Whit like is it?

It's a peatbog, it's a daurk forest.

It's a cauldron o lye, a saltpan or a coal mine.

If you're gey lucky it's a bonny, bricht bere meadow or a park o kye.

Or mibbe... it's a field o stanes.

It's a tenement or a merchant's ha.

It's a hure hoose or a humble cot. Princes Street or Paddy's Merkit.

It's a fistfu o fish or a pickle o oatmeal.

It's a queen's banquet o roast meats and junkets.

It depends. It depends...

Ah dinna ken whit like *your* Scotland is. Here's mines.

National flower: the thistle.

National pastime: nostalgia.

National weather: smirr, haar, drizzle, snaw!

National bird: the crow, the corbie, la corbeille, le corbeau, moi!

How me? Eh? Eh? Eh? Voice like a choked laugh. Ragbag o a burd in ma black duds, aw angles and elbows and broken oxter feathers, black beady een in ma executioner's hood. No braw, but Ah think Ah hae a sort of black glamour?

Do I no put ye in mind of a skating minister, or on the other fit, the parish priest, the durty beast?

My nest's a rickle o sticks.

I live on lamb's eyes and road accidents.

Oh, see, after the battle, after the battle, man, it's a pure feast – ma eyes are ower big even for *my* belly, in lean years o peace, my belly thinks my throat's been cut.

CORBIE *laughs and is suddenly surrounded by the whole* COMPANY *who mill and circle, stop and pose, striking attitudes, looking the audience in the eye – one moment confrontationally, another suspiciously, then the next with the frank and open curiousity of children. Now* CORBIE *takes, from out of their ranks, the twa queens by the hand, parades them like a ringmaster or a barker would a pair of his carnival acts or a cabaret emcee his star burlesque strippers, showing them off.*

Once upon a time there were twa queens on the wan green island, and the wan green island was split intae twa kingdoms. But no *equal* kingdoms, naebody in their richt mind would insist on that.

For the northern kingdom was cauld and sma. And the people were low-statured and ignorant and feart o their lords and poor? They were starvin! And their queen was beautiful and tall and fair and… Frenchified.

The other kingdom in the island was large, and prosperous, with wheat and barley and fat kye in the fields o her yeoman fermers, and wool in her looms, and beer in her barrels and, at the mouth of her greatest river, a great port, a glistening city that sucked all wealth to its centre – which was a palace and a court of a queen. She was a cousin, a clever cousin, a wee bit aulder, and mibbe no sae braw as the other queen, but a queen nevertheless.

Queen o a country wi an army, an a navy and dominion over many lands.

Quick burst of a sad or ironic jig.

Twa queens. Wan green island. And ambassadors and courtiers came from many lands to seek their hauns…

Scene Two

The Suitors

CORBIE, *watching, listening – as she does all the action of the play, always – is scornful and sceptical of the suitability of every proposed match for either queen. Nevertheless she is, always and quite openly, partial. On* MARY*'s, not* ELIZABETH*'s, side.* MARY *and* ELIZABETH *are passed from pillar to post between the entire* COMPANY, *now a motley of* AMBASSADORS, COURTIERS *or* COMMONERS, *with the dizzy queens whirled through their motions by all and sundry. A dance, a mad tango, to music.*

AMBASSADOR 1 (*to* ELIZABETH). To the most esteemed royal court of Her Majesty Queen Elizabeth of England from His Majesty King Philip of Spain, whose hand in marriage –

CORBIE. King Philip of Spain?

ELIZABETH. Our bloody dead sister's widower? We think *not*, Cecil…

ENGLISH COMMONER 1. I 'ates the bastern Spanish Spanish bastards!

ENGLISH COMMONER 2. At least 'e's not bloody *French*!

ELIZABETH. A *king*! We do not think we could marry a king!

AMBASSADOR 2 (*to* MARY). Pray accept this jewelled miniature with a portrait by our esteemed limner, Sanchez Coello, of Don Carlos of Spain, whose bride perhaps…?

CORBIE. The King o Spain's son, Don Carlos?

MARY (*delighted*). A Catholic!

SCOTS COMMONER 1 (*disgusted*). A *Catholic* – well we canny hae that.

SCOTS COMMONER 2. At least he's no *French*!

ELIZABETH. …On the other hand, Cecil, do contrive to keep the ambassador dangling. Do dandle the odd demi-promise, lest Philip o Spain should try to get a nibble… elsewhere!

MARY. A Catholic! At least he is a good Catholic, even if he's not a king in his own right.

ELIZABETH. I cannot allow her to marry a powerful Catholic…

AMBASSADOR 4 (*to* MARY). Félicitations, Madame la plus belle Reine Marie d'Ecosse from Catharine de' Medici, la Reine de France, mère du roi Charles, who wishes you should consider her son *Henri de Valois*.

CORBIE. Henri de Valois?

SCOTS COMMONER 2. Ah'd raither *Spain* nor bliddy France –

MARY. My own Francis's wee brither! But he's no thirteen year aul… How could ma belle-mère think o't?

ENGLISH COMMONER 1. I'm taking bets on it. Pickering! Ten to one it's Pickering for King of England.

ENGLISH COMMONER 2. Pickering, never!

ELIZABETH (*overhearing*). We do not think we could marry a subject!

ENGLISH COMMONER 2. We know what subject *she'd* have –

ENGLISH COMMONER 1. If he hadn't a wife already!

AMBASSADOR 5 (*to* MARY). What think you of the King of Denmark?

AMBASSADOR 3 (*to* ELIZABETH). From the King of Sweden on behalf of his son, Eric –

SCOTS NOBLE 1 (*to* MARY). The Queen should mairry a Hamilton!

SCOTS NOBLE 2. No she shouldnae! She should mairry a Douglas.

SCOTS NOBLE 3. A Gordon!

SCOTS NOBLE 2. By God and she better no!

SCOTS NOBLE 3. Wha says she'll no?

SCOTS NOBLE 2. I dae!

CORBIE. A Lennox-Stewart, that's wha she should mairry!

SCOTS NOBLES 1, 2 *and* 3 *all draw their swords*.

SCOTS NOBLES 1, 2 *and* 3 (*together*). Ower ma deid body!

ELIZABETH. If we, the Queen, were to follow our own nature's inclinations it would be this: we would rather be a beggar woman and single than a queen and married.

AMBASSADOR 6 (*to* ELIZABETH). Archduke Ferdinand of Austria…?

AMBASSADOR 7 (*to* MARY). Archduke Charles of Austria?

AMBASSADOR 6 (*to* MARY). Archduke Ferdinand of Austria?

AMBASSADOR 7 (*to* ELIZABETH). Archduke Charles of Austria?

ELIZABETH. Methinks they do try to play me and my Scotch cousin off against each other. We must keep the Emperor of Austria sure that Charlie or Ferdie will land him the fat salmon, England, until it is too late for him to net the skinny brown trout of Scotland.

AMBASSADOR 2 (*to* MARY). Don Carlos of Spain!

He gives MARY *a miniature. She holds it.*

MARY. Don Carlos, certainly, to judge from his likeness, is very comely…

CORBIE. I hope they dinna tell her the truth!

Note of discord, a beat's freeze as they parody a twisted, grotesque, crippled boy.

MARY. Aye, Don Carlos looks braw… He'd be the most *politik* marriage…

ELIZABETH. Back to Scotland with you, and let it be clearly known by your mistress, that should she marry Don Carlos of Spain, or make any other powerful Catholic match in Europe, then we shall be forced to regard her as our enemy. We shall never recognise her or her progeny as heirs to the throne of England.

SCOTS AMBASSADOR. Your Majesty, Queen Mary has been despairing of pleasing you by her choice of husband, or of you ever granting her right of succession.

ELIZABETH. Despair! Such a mean, unqueenly emotion. Methinks she doth give up hope too easily. Although it might be thought that to ask a monarch to name her own successor were to ask her to embroider her own winding sheet.

SCOTS COMMONER 1. They say Don Carlos isnae a there.

SCOTS COMMONER 2. Neither was her first wan, the Frenchy.

CORBIE. Naw, wi him it wis his baws never drapped! This yin is a pair stutterin slaiverin waggin baw-faced dafty that takes black-oots, and that they hae to chain up when the mune's oot, or e'en the scullery boys are no safe.

MARY. I shall marry Don Carlos of Spain!

ALL. Olé!

Tango ends. Now there are only the two queens left – and CORBIE.

ELIZABETH. Do not really wish to marry? I?

> I will marry. I have said so. I hope to have children, otherwise I shall never marry.

> MARY *and* ELIZABETH *come together on stage but without seeing the other, each in her own separate and different world.*

MARY. Indeed I wish that Elizabeth was a man and I would willingly marry her! And wouldn't that make an end of all debates!

CORBIE. But she isny. Naw, she isny.

> There are two queens on wan island, both o the wan language – mair or less. Baith young… mair or less. Baith mair or less beautiful. Each the ither's nearest kinswoman on earth. And baith queens. Caw. Caw. Caw.

Scene Three

Queens and Maids

CORBIE.
> Ony queen has an army o ladies and maids
> That she juist snaps her fingers tae summon.
> And yet… I ask you, when's a queen a queen
> And when's a queen juist a wummin?

> CORBIE *snaps her fingers,* ELIZABETH *bobs a curtsy, immediately becoming* BESSIE.

MARY. Bessie, do you think she'll meet me?

BESSIE. Aye, Your Majesty, she'll meet wi ye face to face at York, and, you're richt, gin ye talk thegither it'll aw be soarted oot. If ye hunt aw they courtiers an politicians an *men* awa!

CORBIE. She shall never meet you face to face.

MARY. They say she wears my portrait I sent her in that wee jewelled case hangin fae her girdle. And she sent me an emerald.

CORBIE. Oh aye...!

MARY. I'm shivering... Maytime, and it's cauld enough to gie me *chair de poule*! Ah dinna think Ah'll ever understand this country o mine.

BESSIE. The doctor says we have to mak shair you dinna get aw melancholick, Your Majesty.

MARY. Three years! I mind me and the maries oot on deck chitterin in oor fine French frocks, peerin through the glaur o the air for ae glimpse o my kingdom. Three years and I havena seen it yet!

BESSIE. Naw, naw, ye've never seen your country! You've never made your many progresses through the length and breadth o the land!

MARY. The stour o the air clears, then, sherp, a kafuffle atween a Lennox an a Hamilton, a Hamilton and a Douglas...

Haar fae the sea... Cauld... rebecks and chanters, a pretty masque and a goldhaired bairn presents me wi a filigree hert that's fu o golden coins, new minted. Clouds. A flytin fae Knox. Daurkness. A mad poet tries to mak a hoor o me. Wisps... A revel! Smoke... A banquet for the Ambassador new fae Spain. Fog. A bricht affray in the Canongate, a bloody clash at the Butter Tron, a murdered bairn in the Grassmarket, sunshine, and a ragged, starvin crowd o cheerin, cheerin weans jostle to touch ma velvet goon as I go by. My kingdom. Alternately brutal and boring. And I canny mak sense o it at aw.

BESSIE. It's the weather... It's yir sair side. Doctor says we'll hae to gie ye duck eggs whiskit up in wine tae keep the mist o yir melancholia awa.

MARY. It's daein nothin, Bess! The Queen. And I hae nae power tae mak my country flourish.

I want to marry, Bessie, I want to marry and begin my reign at last.

BESSIE. In good time. A guid man in guid time, madam.

CORBIE. Aye, gie her a guid man, she'll gie him a guid time!

And with another snap of her fingers: all change, and BESSIE *is* ELIZABETH, *proud queen, preening, as* MARY *becomes, in that instant, modest and wary* MARIAN, ELIZABETH's *gentlewoman.*

ELIZABETH. Marian, what do they say she is like?

MARIAN. I don't know, madam.

ELIZABETH. Is she fairer than me? What do they say?

MARIAN. They say she is the fairest queen in Scotland, and you are the fairest queen in England, madam.

ELIZABETH *pinches* MARIAN's *cheek and laughs.*

ELIZABETH. And how do you know this?

MARIAN (*laughing nervously*). …Because I heard you ask her envoy, Melville.

ELIZABETH. And what did he say – when I pressed him?

MARIAN. That *you* were the whiter, their queen 'very lusome'.

ELIZABETH. And who is the higher?

MARIAN. She is…

ELIZABETH. Then she is too high.

MARIAN. You told him!

ELIZABETH. What are her other amusements?

MARIAN. She writes poems apparently…

ELIZABETH. Poems? In English?

MARIAN. In French. And… 'in Scots'.

A burst of scornful laughter from both at the very idea.

ELIZABETH. What else?

MARIAN. She… plays on the lute and the virginals.

ELIZABETH. And does she play well?

MARIAN. 'Tolerably well. For a queen.'

They laugh together.

ELIZABETH. And does she dance?

MARIAN. She dances. She dances, though not so high or so disposedly as you, Your Majesty.

They laugh again. A beat's pause.

(*Emboldened.*) Madam, you know I love you well.

ELIZABETH. Yes, Marian, like all good subjects, I hope.

MARIAN. Then, madam, I beg you marry the Earl of Leicester, for there is such scandal, a babble getting louder and louder all the time.

ELIZABETH. They say what, Marian?

MARIAN. Madam, I think you know right well.

ELIZABETH. I cannot imagine what they would say about Us.

MARIAN. Just that… you behave together as if you were married already.

ELIZABETH. We do love him right well, indeed.

MARIAN. And he you – madam, I do not think much heed is paid to the bad things some people say, and if you married…

ELIZABETH. I have always said I shall marry – if I marry – as Queen and not as Elizabeth. You think because my subjects love me as their queen they'll have me marry where I will?

MARIAN. Madam, I know so. Marry my Lord Leicester, and
live in happiness, that England shall be a peaceable
kingdom.

ELIZABETH *holds her breath for a beat. Then smiles.*

CORBIE.
Och, when a queen wad wed,
Or tak a man tae bed,
She only does whit ony maid funns chancy.
So dinna argue the toss,
Just show them wha's boss –
You're the Queen so mairry wha ye fancy.

ELIZABETH (*to herself, considering the bareness of the third
finger of her own left hand*). Robert Dudley, my darling, my
Lord Leicester… my love.

CORBIE.
Aye, in England there's a wild floo'erin love,
That the saicret daurkness nourishes.
But in Scotlan – in the braid daylicht! –
The daurk bloom o *hatred* flourishes.

Scene Four

Knox and Mary

KNOX, *in bowler hat and with umbrella, marching. Two
members of the* COMPANY, *stamping, sway a banner behind
him, and all the* COMPANY *swagger with exaggerated
Orangemen's gait. Flute music and hoochs and ugly skirls.*

KNOX. I, John Knox, do preach the evangel of Jesus Christ
Crucified, by repentance and faith. And justification by faith
alone. Moved by my God and in humble obedience to Him
wha is abune us aw, I hae been commandit to blaw the first
blast o the trumpet against the monstrous regiment o women,

an abomination against nature and before God; and to disclose unto this, my realm, the vanity and iniquity of the papistical religion and all its pestilent manifestations in Sodom priesthooses and poxetten nunneries.

A roll of bread is placed upon a bare table. MARY *and* KNOX *sit with the fact of it between them. Others fall back, listen, watch – and move their lips in prayer.*

MARY. John Knox, mair nor three years I hae borne wi you in aw your rigorous manners o speakin oot, baith against masel and ma French uncles. And yit I hae socht your favour by aw possible means.

KNOX. When it shall please God to deliver you frae that bondage of darkness and error into the one true religion, Your Majesty shall find the liberty o my tongue as a soothing balm unto ye. For, inside the preaching place, madam, I am not master of myself but the mere instrument of Him wha commands me to speak plain and flatter no flesh upon the face of the earth, nor wait on the courts o princes or the chaummers o ladies.

MARY. But what have ye to do with my marriage? What are ye in this commonwealth?

KNOX. A subject born within the same. Albeit I be neither earl, lord nor baron within it. But, however low and abject I am in your eyes, it is ma duty no less to forewarn of what I foresee hurtin it than I were o the nobility.

And gin the nobility should consent ye marry ony husband wha isna o the one true faith then they do as muckle as lies within their power to renounce Christ, to betray the freedom of the realm – and, in the end, to do small comfort to yourself.

CORBIE. Corbie says, by the bones of your beloved mother you must destroy this man! Knox, nox as black as nicht, nox lik a the bitter pousons, nox lik three fearfu chaps at the door, did ding her doon! Knox did lead the rebels. Knox did break yer mither's hert and Knox did laugh when she did dee.

Hark at him: 'The Guid Lord says – and I agree wi him!'
Ach! Hark. Cark!

MARY. Maister Knox, I see in you yin wha is convincit he be
moved by love of God, but is in truth fired raither by hatred o
mankind.

CORBIE. Cark! Aye, tell him!

KNOX. There is yin abune us aw, madam, wha is the best
judge, the only.

MARY. You raised up a part of this nation – ma subjects –
against ma mither, and against me, their prince, anointed by
God. You hae written a treasonous treatise o a book against
ma just authority. You have been the cause of great sedition
and greater slaughter in England –

KNOX. By the richt worshipping of God, men learn from their
hearts to obey their just princes.

MARY. But ye think that I hae nae just authority?

KNOX. Your Majesty, if this realm finds no inconveniency in
the regiment o a woman, then that which they approve I shall
not further disallow.

MARY. Except within your own heart and breast?

KNOX. My heart is God's. But I shall be as weill content to live
under ye as Paul was tae live under Nero.

MARY. Sae ye will gie to *Caesar-ina* whit is Caesar-ina's?

KNOX. I see madam kens her scriptures.

MARY. I ken ma scriptures. I hae baith heard and read. (*Pause*.)
Maister Knox, because I am by nature douce, and queyet,
dinna think I hae nae convictions or beliefs locked in ma
silent heart – though I dae not *trumpet* them abroad.

KNOX. Well! If I did blaw the first blast of the trumpet,
madam, against the monstrous regiment o women – this blast
was neither against your person or your regiment, but against
that bloody Jezebel o England!

MARY. I am shair my guid cousin Elizabeth would be maist disconcertit to ken Maister Knox, wha doth profess the same faith as she, cried her a Jezebel!

KNOX. The Jezebel is Bloody Mary before her, as weel you ken! Wha did practise murderous and several slaughter amang the hedgerows, till the vera weans o the serfs o the loyal lords wha did profess the true faith, did lie wi their guts aw skailt oot amang the stubble o the field, while the air was stinkan and corruptit wi the thick smoke fae the fires o burning martyrs and ministers o the truth.

Madam, open yir heart to God's truth –

MARY. – And you will bid my subjects obey me?

KNOX. Madam, I will.

MARY. Then they shall obey you and not me. Their lawful prince. Like I say, Maister Knox, I hae heard and read.

KNOX. So, madam, did the Jews wha crucified Christ Jesus read both the law and the prophets – and interpretit them as suitit themsels.

MARY. And do ye no interpret as suits you?

KNOX. I believe only what God plainly speaks in His word.

MARY. And yet the same words sound vera different to my ears.

KNOX, *during next, takes the bread, crumbles it, scorns it, desecrates it in* MARY*'s eyes.*

KNOX. For instance: the Mass.

A God of Bread. A god o breid, it is idolatory! Nay, I say that it is *mair* idolatory tae mak a god of breid than when the heathens in their daurkness made fause idols. Consider a god o wood or a god o stane – well, a god o bread is mair miserable… This god will putrify in a single season. The rain or snow can mak saps o sicc a god. Ony durty maid in a scullery can mak a god tae rise in a warm an yeasty corner!

Rats and mice will require nae better dinner than roon white gods enough! Show me in the Bible whaur Christ Jesus at His Last Supper did command the Mass? – I tell you, nae mention is made o sicc in aw the scripture.

MARY. Ye are ower sair for me!

She breaks down sobbing. He is astonished, even sorry.

KNOX. Madam, in God's presence I swear that I never delightit in the weeping of ony o God's creatures. As I can scarcely staun the tears o my ain wife or ma ain young sons when ma ain haund is forcit to correct them, faur less can I rejoice in the greetin and howlin and bawlin o Yir Majesty.

He goes to touch her. She recoils.

But I hae tae thole your saut tears, rather than I betray my God or nation by my silence.

MARY. Yet will I in my realm and in ma heart silently defend the Kirk o Rome. And I will marry wha I please. Ye will grant to me guid tolerance – as I hae *aye* granted to you and your Reformit Kirk.

KNOX. Madam, I shall never be seduced by the Siren song o Toleration. I fear you dinnae understaun this country ye are queen o.

KNOX *goes to bow out, having said enough. But –*

MARY. Nevertheless, I will marry wha I please!

KNOX *has to have the Last Word.*

KNOX. I pray God grant you the wisdom of Deborah among the Israelites.

Exit KNOX. MARY, shaking, is left alone on her knees, praying.

CORBIE. Gin ye want to gag Maister Knox you will hae tae abolish the Mass and embrace his cauld kirk.

MARY. And is there nae comfort in his kerque?

CORBIE. Aye. Cauld comfort. But there are those wha say it a the better suits the climate.

MARY. And you think gin I sat on St Giles's hard pews on a Sunday I'd sit surer oan ma ain throne aw week lang?

CORBIE. Nae doot aboot that!

He has cowped the Queen o Heaven so how could he worry aboot cowpin a mere earthly queen?

MARY. Then the Protestants dinnae love oor Blessed Virgin?

CORBIE. Knox has torn the Mother of God from oot the sky o Scotland and has trampit her celestial blue goon amang the muck and mire and has blotted oot every name by which ye praise her – Stella Maris, Star of the Sea, Holy Mother, Notre Dame, Oor Lady o Perpetual Succour.

MARY. But, if he hae torn her frae the blue sky, what has he left in her place?

CORBIE. A black hole, a jaggit gash, *naethin*.

MARY. But how should I live without Our Lady?

CORBIE. Easy. You hae livit withoot yir earthly mother, sae ye can live without your heavenly yin.

MARY *considers this for a moment, but – defiantly – back at* CORBIE:

MARY. I will marry wha I can love!

CORBIE *turns to the audience. She gives up, she really does.*

CORBIE. Oh, in the name o the Wee Man…

In the name of the Faither, the Son, the Power and the Glory,

I wish to Christ I could tell yez a Different Story!

Scene Five

Repressed Loves (The First)

CORBIE.

> Sae oor queen, wha'd 'rule by gentleness',
> Is but a pair fendless craiture –
> An in Englan the Lass-Wha-Was-Born-To-Be-King
> Maun dowse her womanische nature.

ELIZABETH is alone, lying down, asleep, dreaming. She rolls over, moaning and murmuring, then wakes up with a scream –

ELIZABETH. Robert!

Awake, sobbing and crying. Enter MARIAN, running.

MARIAN. Bad dreams. Bad dreams again, Your Majesty, hush…

ELIZABETH. Mum was… Dad was… Dad was there, I was only tiny and… my… dolly's head… fell off. Then it changed the way it does in dreams and Leicester, well, we were just two little children playing in the woods, but I knew the way you do that it was really I and my Robert and… then long empty corridors I was all alone and a crown rolling…

She cries again.

MARIAN. Hush! Hot milk and honey, I'll –

But ELIZABETH detains her, cries some more, then calms.

ELIZABETH. I couldn't have married him, Marian.

MARIAN. Well… no, madam. Perhaps not.

ELIZABETH. I told him! I said, 'Leicester, if I married you and we lay down together as King and Queen, then we should wake as plain Mister and Mistress Dudley. The Nation would not have it.'

MARIAN. Surely the scandal would have died down? Can't you marry him secretly and –

ELIZABETH. She trumped us. His bloody wife. Why couldn't she let him decently divorce her? Oh no, she has to commit suicide. Now everyone is sure he murdered her. If he'd bloody murdered her, he'd have done it a lot better than that. Made quite sure it looked as though she took her own life.

MARIAN. Marry him secretly! In six months... a year... everyone will have forgotten she ever lived.

ELIZABETH. Too late! I've told him I want him to marry Madam o Scots.

MARIAN. ...Who?

ELIZABETH. Queen Mary, and take him off to Edinburgh.

MARIAN. Madam!

ELIZABETH. Why not? I hear she is very attractive, though I've yet to set eyes on her.

MARIAN. But, madam –

ELIZABETH. Oh yes! Bit on the tall side, of course, and hair that reddish colour that makes the complexion sickly-looking – oh, and a virgin too, although she has been married. Altogether doing it exactly the wrong way round for my taste, but still, she is a queen after all, so –

MARIAN. – He loves you!

ELIZABETH. I'm sure she'll make him happy, that'll shut all their mouths and we'll have a loyal Englishman – I think we may depend on him to remain a loyal Englishman? – In her bed. Well, we really cannot have her married in France again, else the French King can straddle England with one foot in Calais, the other in Edinburgh, and piss down on us all fire, brimstone and poison. Besides, I have already broached it with the Scotch Ambassador.

MARIAN *looks on her with amazement.* ELIZABETH *suddenly crumbles and she is sobbing again. Taking her life in her hands,* MARIAN *holds her, hushes her tentatively.*

No more. What shall it profit a woman if she can rule a whole kingdom but cannot quell her own rebellious heart?

Robert, you were more dangerous to me than a thousand, thousand Northern Catholics, poised and armed. I am not proud I love him – but I am proud that, loving him, still I would not let him master me.

Repressed Loves (The Second)

CORBIE. Aye, very good, Queen Bess! Thon's a quine wi her heid screwed oan. An Mary…? Well, I've said it afore an I'll say it again:

> When a queen wud wed,
> Or tak a man tae bed,
> She only does whit *ony* maid funns chancy.
> Dinnae argue the toss,
> Juist show them wha's boss –
> You're the Queen so mairry wha ye fancy.

Enter BOTHWELL, *bowing, cap in hand.*

MARY. Alison Craik, Earl Bothwell!

BOTHWELL. Wha?

CORBIE. He kens her!

MARY. You ken her!

BOTHWELL. Dae I?

MARY. I ken you dae.

BOTHWELL. Well, Your Majesty, you ken, I dinna ken aw the lassies I ken. So mibbe you ken mair than I dae…

MARY. Alison Craik is the dochter of thon respectable Edinburgh merchant, whase hoose near the Saut Tron ye did rudely invade and enter, ye and ma pair auld uncle d'Elboeuf aw fired up wi drink and his brains addled.

BOTHWELL. Oh, *that* Alison…

MARY. Ma pair gyte auld uncle, Bothwell!

BOTHWELL. Aye, his auld hurdies werena fit to gang whaur his new-youthfu and fair French-style fancies would have led him tae lie…

CORBIE. Caw! Caw!

MARY. Ye led him to wickedness, Bothwell! Drunkenness and rapine, Ah'll no hae it!

BOTHWELL. Ah dinna expect ye'll get offert it vera often. No in your station in life.

CORBIE. Caw! Caw canny.

MARY. *Nobody* speaks to the Queen like that!

BOTHWELL. An that's juist wha Ah am. Naebody. Ah widnae let naebody bother you, Your Majesty.

MARY. Apparently you are naebody. Naebody to be chidit by the Kirk Assembly. The excellent Protestants were vera quick tae complain and denounced fae the pulpit ma pair auld uncle wha couldna go whaur you didna lead him. And did they chide you?

BOTHWELL. Noo, wha are you worrit aboot – your auld uncle or… the fair Alison.

MARY. I want, in my realm, Maister Hepburn O'Bothwell, that women should sleep sound in their beds.

CORBIE. You tell him!

BOTHWELL. Because dinna, you ken. Worry aboot Alison. She's juist a tail.

MARY *gasps*.

A brass nail, a hure, a daw, a penny-jo. (*Pause.*) Oh, a *pricey* penny-jo, her faither *is* a city merchant. (*Pause.*) Sleepin sound isny lik Alison, if aw I've heard be true... Though, mind, she sleeps the sleep o the just. The just-keistit that is.

No that I've a bad word for ony lass that is an honest hure. But Alison Craik is the Earl o Arran's hure. And the Earl o Arran is a bloody Hamilton... So I had her.

She wisna unwilling.

She wisna unwilling, but yir auld uncle d'Elboeuf wisna able... Sae the Kirk Assembly are makkin a mountain oot o a mowdie-hill. At least in nuncle d'Elby-boeuf's case...

MARY (*wearily*). 'Because he is a Hamilton!' Ah'll no have you nobles o this yin nation aye at each ither's throats lik terriers.

BOTHWELL. Well, madam, I fear you are queen o the wrang kintra. Terriers we are, it is our nature. Be a while afore ye make kittocky kittlin-cats o us, or wee saft-moothed spaniels to stick oor heids in yer lap and fawn ower each ither while we wait for yir favours.

MARY. I'm your queen. And in three years in this country I canna depend on any o ye to show me royal respect as I am due, although in every way I try – (*She dissolves into shaming tears.*)

CORBIE. Don't greet!

BOTHWELL. Madam: I hae the greatest respect for my anointed queen, whase grace and beauty gladdens my heart and whase gentleness and clemency does tame my savagery.

CORBIE. Aye well, there's mibbe somethin tae be said for weepin...

BOTHWELL. – And whase courage and swiftness in the chase does quicken my spirit and speed my ain steed in pursuivance of the quarry.

MARY. I didna ken ye took such pleasure in hunting.

BOTHWELL. In the chase? Aye. When there's a fine white hind dancin afore me through the trees, and I glisk it, then lose it again, glisk it, lose it… but my hound, my pointing hound, doth throw back his liver-coloured chops and bay. Because my hound and I can smell it. Glintin through the trees in the gloamin daurk.

Hunting? Aye. When I am honoured to be in the Queen's party.

Hae we no shared minny's an exhaustin day's sport, Your Majesty? And yet ye turned me doon.

I humbled masel but still you widna mairry me…

A long beat between them.

MARY. Nae mair Alison Craiks!

BOTHWELL (*bowing*). Your Majesty.

MARY. Nae mair tiltin at Hamiltons.

BOTHWELL. – But, Your Majesty, there is a history to this dispute!

MARY. I dinna want to hear your history!

Doom. A drumbeat.

Bothwell, as well as Queen, I am widow. And maiden. And I would hae all unprotectit women in my realm honoured in their privacy!

BOTHWELL. I ken. You are heart-sorry for Alison Craik.

MARY. And I tell you, if there is any mair of this I will be forcit to outlaw you, to put you to the horn!

CORBIE. Caw!

BOTHWELL Put me to the horn would you, my leddy? I tell you, Ah'll pit you to the horn and you'd be gled to rin outlawed wi me.

MARY. Bothwell! –

BOTHWELL. Nae mair tiltin at Alison Craik. Nor at Arran the Hamilton gin he gree no tae tilt at me.

MARY. Go then. And keep the peace, James Hepburn, I charge you, keep peace.

He bows out. BESSIE, *as she comes in, passes him, bristles.*

Bessie! Bessie, do you think it's true he is a warlock?

BESSIE. A warlock, Your Majesty, why?

MARY. He frichtens me.

BESSIE. Aye, madam, but Ah dinna think there is anythin eldritch or extraordinar in tha...

MARY. But how then would he hae the power tae disturb me so?

BESSIE *thinks better of trying to reply.*

CORBIE (*a mutter*). Well, Bessie, ma lass, there's nae answer tae that, eh?

Scene Six

Elizabeth Stirs It Up

CORBIE, *in a 'let's get a move on' fashion, snaps her fingers in her shape-changeing, scene-changing way.* BESSIE *becomes proud Queen* ELIZABETH *again, and* MARY *maid* MARIAN.

CORBIE.
>   Aye, a man he is a tasty dish,
>   But mairriage is a kettle o fish...
>   Twa queens, ae nicht, push their plates awa,
>   When they sit doon tae sup.
>   Yin doesnae ken whit's steerin her –
>   Yin doesnae ken whit tae steer up!

ELIZABETH *is speaking to* MARIAN *in a conspiratorial whisper.*

ELIZABETH. He is here, Marian?

MARIAN. Yes, madam.

ELIZABETH. And none saw him who could carry tales to my Lord Leicester?

MARIAN. I think not, madam...

ELIZABETH. Go then, send him in...

DARNLEY, *young and nervous, enters, kneels.*

Cousin!

DARNLEY. Your Majesty.

ELIZABETH. Do get up, let me look at you. Well, I haven't seen you since you were but a beardless boy – and now you are grown such a fine long lad. How old are you?

DARNLEY. Nineteen, madam, almost –

ELIZABETH. Old enough, eh? Cousin, the Scotch Ambassador and I have been discussing you lately, wondering whether we are to allow you to take yourself off to Bonnie Scotland. What think you?

DARNLEY. Madam, I don't know what to say, you surprise me so!

ELIZABETH. Oh nonsense! You know how your Mama Lennox has been two-three years a-wheedling at me. 'Will I – pretty-please will I, oh Your Maj – help her to restore your father and your sire to his rightful lands and estate in Scotland?'

What do you suppose your mother really wants?

DARNLEY. Madam, I know she desires nothing more than justice for my father, an end to his banishment from his own homeland. He's an old man, Your Majesty.

ELIZABETH. Oh, we're all old to you, Henry.

DARNLEY. Twenty years! Since before I was even born. Exiled, unfairly stripped of his lands by the Scottish Crown.

ELIZABETH. Yes, yes, and of course your mam wants him to die happy and be buried on his own soil. Commendable, such uxoriousness.

He doesn't understand.

That means nice-little-wifeyness, Henry. Do sit down, Henry!

Henry, your mama and I are both grandchildren of Henry the Seventh of England. You are aware of that?

DARNLEY. Yes, of course, ma'am.

ELIZABETH. There are even some who say she has a close claim to succeed me.

DARNLEY. Madam, I think you know my mother is your most loyal and most humble subject.

ELIZABETH (*too quickly*). Even though she is a Catholic like the Scotch bitch! (*Recovers.*) Perhaps.

Oh, Henry, some of my advisors and statesmen are very suspicious sorts of people, you know I really cannot keep up with them! They try to convince me your mother has big ambitions for her little son, and before Queen Mary's poor wee French runt had begun to rot in his coffin, Mum had sent you and your brother off on French holidays, a-commiserating with the young widow.

DARNLEY. I was but a child then!

ELIZABETH. So was she, Henry, but you're both all growed up now.

But I know, dear, you would never think to marry a lady so much older than you.

DARNLEY. – Only three years!

ELIZABETH. Ah yes, but, Henry, when the difference is the wrong way round and the maid is older than the man, it puts the balance out of kilter. Don't think of it! You are a right loyal subject of England, Henry Darnley?

DARNLEY. Madam, you know I am.

ELIZABETH. Exactly. I will tell my ministers so! I'll explain it all to them – the old dad, etcetera. I think you may depend on it, we will allow you to go.

DARNLEY. My father will be –

ELIZABETH. Except –

DARNLEY. Ma'am?

ELIZABETH. Well… can I trust you to keep a confidence? Maybe I shouldn't tell you this but… you see, negotiations are well advanced with the Scotch Ambassador that Queen Mary will marry my Lord Leicester.

DARNLEY. Leicester, but he is your…

ELIZABETH. My favourite! Yes. Well, do they say so? Perhaps. But wise monarchs should keep no favourites. I am determined there shall be no other English rival to Leicester for the hand of the Queen of Scots. And it's been troubling me a little, just in case – no fault of your own – but what if the Scotch Queen should take it into her head to prefer *you*, being there, to *him*, being here? You do see my little difficulty? Remember, when you are in Scotland you'll be beyond my power. Why, you could pretend to be a Catholic yourself and woo her, and me not able to stop you! Honestly, were I not so confident of your loyalty, I could not let you go.

It slowly sinks in that she is saying yes.

DARNLEY. May I?

ELIZABETH. I've signed the paper already. You may go. And… you may go!

DARNLEY. Your Majesty. (*Bowing, he begins to leave.*)

ELIZABETH. Young Henry, be careful, I hear it's a cold, dire, rough place. Worse than Yorkshire.

Scene Seven

Mary Queen of Scots' Progress, The Bairns, and John Knox's Shame

CORBIE *shivers. In the cold, and more than that. Shakes herself though, to drive her story forward, as she must.*

CORBIE.
>Though the wind blaws snell doon the Canongate the day,
>There's ne'er an honest bairn nor a rogue less,
>As through the toun, in fine processioun,
>Comes the Queen, and her cooncil, in progress.

Bright processional music. The COMPANY *are now a ragamuffin, shilpit, poor-looking selection of the Edinburgh common people; gadges, bairns, dafties and auld folk. They might join in with* CORBIE's *next verse –*

>Gaberlunzies in duds and pair drabs in their rags,
>Can feast their een on hoo the Queen and the court dress,
>Though wir teeth micht chitter we dinna feel bitter –
>Naw, we cheer at *Queen Mary's progress*!

They do, raucously. MARY *is now* MAIRN, *a wee poor Scottish beggar lass, and* ELIZABETH *is* LEEZIE, *her tarty wee companion. All are cheering and watching the (to us) invisible progess as it passes them.*

MAIRN. The Queen! The Queen! She's comin.

LEEZIE. Aw, she's beautiful, eh, Mairn?

MAIRN. Lovely.

LEEZIE. Mind you, we'd be braw in braw claes...

MAIRN. Ah don't think Ah could lukk lik the Queen, Leezie...

LEEZIE. Aye ye could, if yer frock wis French flamin velvet wi a siller-lace collar.

Suddenly a shower of small coins – like those thrown by custom to the local kids at a Scots wedding as the bridal car leaves.

ALL. Scrammle! It's a scrammle! Haw, it's mines! (*Etc.*)

– and they are squabbling and fighting over every last round coin of it.

KNOX *looks on in disgust.*

KNOX. And thus are oor pair, fair bairns o Scotland reduced to fechtin ower trashy scraps o glisterin tin coins that French hoor scatters fae her progress. By smilin an dauncin does she steal the people's hearts away from the true priests and the true religion. Starvin. The people are starvin. But inasmuch as they hunger for earthly sustenance, a hundredfold were they famisht for the spiritual food of true redemption. Till the Lord God did deliver them.

Everybody except KNOX, LEEZIE *and* MAIRN *disappears.* LEEZIE *and* MAIRN *are rolling on the ground among the dirt, laughing. Under* LEEZIE's *bold prompting and nudging,* MAIRN *is soon staring at* KNOX.

LEEZIE. He wis. He wis starin. Gaun. Ask him, Mairn!

MAIRN. Dinna, Leezie, dinna. Ah canny.

LEEZIE. Starin ett ye. He'll ken ye the next time, honestly. Haw! Lukks lik he's juist back frae a funeral! He'll be definitely wantin a wee bit rumplefyke then… (*Shouts.*) Haw, maister, ma pal wants tae ken if ye want tae go wi her?

MAIRN. Come awa, Leezie…

KNOX. Awa tae hell wi ye, ya jauds!

MAIRN. Leezie! Leezie, yon's… John Knox! Ow-ah!

LEEZIE. Maister, buy us wir denner…?

KNOX. Awa and pray the Lord tae forgive ye. You're nobbut weans!

LEEZIE. Well, yon's no whit ye said last week!

She runs off, wild coarse laughter, a rude sign, a flashed bum, a bent arm. KNOX is right at scared wee MAIRN, facing her down and everything freezes. LEEZIE is far off from them, frozen in her cheeky running away; MAIRN suddenly straight and tall, suddenly totally MARY the Queen in KNOX's eyes – as he chides a cheeky wee harlot on the cauld Canongate.

KNOX's hand is raised in anger but stayed in awe.

KNOX. By Christ. Ah'll tan yir arse fur ye, ya wee hoor o Babylon. Lukk at ye! Wi yir lang hair lik a flag in the wind, an advertisement o lust tae honest men. An, ach, they big roon een lik a dumb animal, slinkan alang the road wi yir hurdies hingin oot yir sark, an yon smell aff ye, ya durty wee fork-arsed bitch, ye.

Nae wunder it is written in the Guid Book that your kind are the very gate and port o the devil – Ah'll leave the rid mark o ma haun on your white flesh afore Ah –

By an effort of pure will, that moment of lust, madness and ambiguity passes and KNOX is back in control of himself.

Awa and behave! Pray God forgive you and sin nae mair.

CORBIE (*singing*).
    In papische days wi evil ways,
    The sinner sins and then he pays.
    The blind bishop –

ALL (*joining in*).
    – The blind bishop he canna preach,
    For playin wi the lasses.
    The friar flatters aw in reach,
    For alms that they possesses.
    The curate his creed, he canna read –
    But noo we are reformit.

> Hoo shall the meenister creesh his palms,
> Or his cauld bed be warmit?

BOTHWELL *comes now, urgently, to* KNOX.

BOTHWELL. A wee burd tells me the Queen isna pleased wi you! Well, you arena feart, ma freen, speakin oot lik yon!

KNOX. The marriage o our queen is in all men's mouths, Bothwell, sae it is ma duty to denounce France and decry Spain and to preach against allowin her a papish marriage. For by the same act o takkin a man tae her bed, she maks a king tae a people.

We, the people, should choose a husband fur a lassie raither than a silly wee furrin lassie should choose a king for a people.

BOTHWELL. Well, you tell her! You arena feart…

KNOX. Why should the pleasin face o a gentlewoman affray me? I hae lookit in the faces o many angry men and no been afraid, no above measure.

BOTHWELL. Well, Ah'm mair feart o a pleasin female face nor an angry male yin ony day. No that I'd ever let a quine ken it. They're lik dugs – show them fear and they are forcit tae bite ye.

KNOX. She's only a silly spilte wee French lassie, Bothwell.

BOTHWELL. Only a silly spilte wee French lassie wha could cowp the kirk and cut your heid aff, John Knox.

KNOX. She's only a queen.

BOTHWELL (*as they begin to exit*). And what's a queen?

KNOX. Juist a silly, spilte wee lassie.

Scene Eight

Darnley and a Fever

CORBIE.
> Yestreen the Queen was wyce enough,
> To forswear all desire,
> From love, and the keist-and-rummle o love,
> She flinched, as at fire.
>
> But noo… the Queen and Lord Darnley!
> Close-closeted thegither,
> Young Lord Darnley's on his sickbed –
> But baith o them hae a fever!

DARNLEY in bed, MARY by his bedside with a bowl of soup.

DARNLEY. Your Majesty, is it you?

MARY. Yes, it's me. It's Mary.

DARNLEY. This is humiliating.

MARY. Wheesht!

DARNLEY. Measles! A childhood complaint, it's –

MARY. I had it in France when I was a wee, wee girl!

DARNLEY. You poor little thing, so far away from your mother too.

MARY. Aye. I grat full sore for her.

DARNLEY. I don't know how she could have sent you away. You must have been such a pretty child.

MARY. I dinna ken boot that. But I missed her.

> She had to dae it though, to keep me safe an soond. There were plenty plots to steal the infant Queen and rule in her stead.

If I had a child though… oh, I dinna think I could send ma ain bairn awa.

DARNLEY. Poor Mary!

MARY. Oot on the deck, ready tae embark, an Ah wis sae excitit – I'm a great sailor, ye ken, I wis the only wan no seeck aw the wey tae France – but, ma mither, she wis greetin an roarin and stitchin wee medals o the Blessed Virgin intae ma claes tae keep me safe…

I didna ken whit was the maitter. I didna realise hoo lang it'd be ere I'd see her again.

DARNLEY. My mother's a Catholic too!

MARY. Is she?

DARNLEY. Oh yes.

I can't imagine my mother ever sending me away!

MARY. No even for your ain guid?

DARNLEY. I don't think so. (*Laughing.*) I'm glad she's not here now, she'd be rushing around with junkets and milk jellies and broth to get my strength back up!

MARY. I brocht you some broth! I forgot! That wis why I came! It'll be cauld noo, I'll go get some mair.

DARNLEY. Mary, don't – I'm not hungry!

MARY. Do ye not want onything?

DARNLEY. No. Just… stay with me, Mary.

Long beat. They look deep into each other's eyes.

CORBIE. Ach, here we go…

A burst of ironic music segues into –

ELIZABETH. And really it has proved remarkably simple. All we had to do was keep it nice and complicated. Well, once Philip withdrew Don Carlos – although clearly the boy was an idiot, even Mary couldn't have married him – well, we pushed for Leicester, hinted we might be about to ratify on the succession question, *if* we got her married to an Englishman and a Protestant... but, alack, our heart was not in it.

A weakness of course, must be a bit of the old *dad* in me, must cut it out.

But, secretly, we were somewhat relieved when the old religion bit was a little too much for Mary to swallow. Well, we might have got somewhere if Master Knox could have been persuaded to be a little less confrontational – really there is no *moderation* in the man – but, truth to tell, I was glad really when she would have none of my Robert.

Then the measles! What a stroke of luck, poor Darnley all flushed and fevered, and Queen Mary playing nursemaid, brought out her tender feelings, most affecting... And now they are to be married. All it took was for me to *expressly* forbid it and he was irresistible.

Which should keep her busy at home sorting out the snarls and quarrels that lad'll cause among her nobility! Too busy to indulge in any mischief among *my* Disenchanted Catholics.

And it does let my Lord Leicester off the hook. Pity, really. There were no more *piquant* nights than those ones he were never sure if he were off to the *Tower* or to *Scotland* in the morning.

Scene Nine

A Wedding

Music. Solemn and processional. Celebratory. Erotic.

As MARY *and* DARNLEY *enter, robed for their wedding –*

CORBIE (*singing*).
>Oor queen has mairrit her a knight,
>His curls are fair as ony child,
>Sma is his mooth and his manner douce,
>His eyes are meek and mild.
>
>Oor queen has mairrit her a knight,
>She fondles him an he were her pet,
>He moves sae spry and his voice sae high –
>Yon long lad he is a-growin yet…
>
>Oor queen has mairrit her a knight,
>His cheek as saft as ony baby boy,
>Soon may she declare a son and heir,
>To be oor nation's joy.

COMPANY *all join in with the song and the ceremony.*

ALL. And we hae made to them a bed.
>We made it large and wide,
>That Mary oor queen and the Lord Darnley,
>Micht lay doon side by side.

MARY. And each o ye draw oot a pin,
>A pin frae oot ma mournin gear,
>Alas, alack, in weeds o black,
>To show I hae a widow been,
>And ever sin I hae been wrapped in,
>Ma mournin gear, ma mournin gear,
>For many a long and weary year.

And I shall loose ma lang rid hair,
Ungimp ma girdles o the plaited silk,
Slip frae ma sark and in the dark,
Ma bodie will gleam as white as milk.

And I shall be dressed in nakedness,
My briests twa aiples o desire,
And you shall hae the brichtest jewel,
That nestles in my brooch o red-gowd wire.

MARY *and* DARNLEY *kiss*.

Blackout.

End of Act One.

ACT TWO

Scene One

Seigneur Riccio, a Fortune, a Baby, and a Big Baby

The clattering noise of an old typewriter. Lights come up to reveal RICCIO, typing away efficiently, with MARY pacing, dictating. Fast, secretive, well-established hard work. RICCIO has a slight hunchback, is small and slight but with a face both beautiful and gentle in his twisted body. CORBIE snaps her fingers.

MARY. Twa copies, Seigneur Davy, yin tae the Papal Nuncio, yin tae the Cardinal o Lorraine – ssh! Carefu, carefu, no a word tae naebody, no tae the King, no even tae Bothwell.

RICCIO puts his fingers to his lips, smiles.

RICCIO. Puoi avere fiducia in me, Davy Riccio!

He goes back to typing. MARY sits down and looks at her belly.

MARY. Please mak it be true, mak it a richt enough. And mak it a boy – for your ain sake.

RICCIO looks at her, shakes his head and wags his finger, goes on typing.

CORBIE. And is that what we'd expect to see, no three month eftir yir weddin? Whaur's yir bonny young groom? Eh? Eh?

RICCIO rips out the sheet of paper, takes it over to MARY, who plucks a feather out of CORBIE's coat sleeve and signs flamboyantly.

MARY. And you hae the stamp we hae made up o the King's signature?

RICCIO *produces it with a flourish and rubber-stamps each paper with a thump.*

Aye… oan the richt-hand side, o coorse. *Mine* must aye hae the pride o place, because it is the name you read first! On the left. (*Pause.*) Oh, Riccio, Riccio, you dinnae think it was… *petty* o me to withdraw the silver ryal?

RICCIO *comes and starts massaging her temples.*

Na, I dinna think so, there was nae choice, Davy. I couldna allow it as a coin o the realm.

CORBIE *does a trick, conjures up one of these very coins.*

CORBIE. The silver ryal, a commemorative coin worth thirty shillings, Scots, to celebrate the love of King Henry for Queen Mary –

CORBIE *bites the coin, testing the metal.*

– Is it genuine?

MARY. The damnable cheek of it – *Henricus* et Maria, Deo Gratia *Rex* et Regina Scotorum! Wrang order.

CORBIE. Whom God hath jined together let nae man cast asunder.

And the coin is turned by a trick magically into two.

MARY. I wish Henry widna harp and carp aboot the crown matrimonial aw the time, for it widna be politick to grant him it.

CORBIE. Even if you wanted tae.

MARY. So, Henry Darnley, you hae nae richt to ma throne eftir ma death – even if it werena for *you*, ma son.

If you *are* a son. Och, I widna wish for ye to be a lassie. Whit think ye, Davy Riccio, boy or girl?

RICCIO *shuts MARY's eyes, leans her back, takes a ring on a ribbon from his pocket and swings it like a pendulum above her belly.*

CORBIE. Whit is't then? Widdershins an it's a boy!

RICCIO waits as the ring swings and stops, then cheekily makes a wee wiggling baby's penis of his crooked little finger at his crotch.

RICCIO. Ragazzo!

MARY. Thank God, a son.

CORBIE. Funny! Yesterday it went the *other* wey and *still* ye said, oh aye it wis a laddie! Dowsers an diviners an fortune-tellers, ever noticed how they aw tell ye whit they think ye want to hear?

MARY. Make him strang! (*Pause.*) Davy Riccio – tell ma fortune!

CORBIE. Ta-rocco!

Tarot cards, outsize, appear. RICCIO spreads them in a circle.

MARY. Only you, Davy, only you said I wis richt to marry Henry Darnley. You cast ma cairts for me – an you chartit ma birth staurs – time an again we turnt up the same cairt...

RICCIO (*turning it up, announcing it yet again*). Gli Amanti!

MARY. The lovers. Numero six. 'A choice.' Except there wis nae choice at aw, you kennt that! Though even *ye* couldna hae fortellt the anger o ma nobles! Damn them aw! Damn England for harbouring the bloody rebels, I'll depend on France and Spain afore England, I'll show them aw I was richt tae follow ma destiny an marry the man I loved.

CORBIE. Lov-*ed*. Note the past tense.

MARY. Noo, Davy, we hae tae cast three, is that no richt?

First card.

MARY *and* RICCIO. Il diavolo!

Second card.

RICCIO. Numero tredici –

MARY (*shivering*). The unnamed card…

RICCIO. La morte.

MARY *tries to laugh it off.*

MARY. Ah ken that's supposed to be a lucky caird, dinna cairds aye mean the opposite? But it frichts me aw the same!

CORBIE. A skeleton wi a grin as wide his ain scythe. Airms and legs in the broken earth. A crowned head, cut aff, in the boattom corner. Only a picture! Colourt in ower crudely by some Admon Kadmon trickster at a tally fair! La morte!

MARY *and* RICCIO (*as the third card goes down*). Justizia!

MARY. Justice, well yon's a lucky caird, eh, Davy?

CORBIE. Oh aye, an – lik chance – it'd be a fine thing.

RICCIO *smiles, soothes, massages her feet and ankles, the original reflexologist.*

CORBIE *picks up the rest of the pack. She fans them.*

An whit else is in here? There's… the world, il mondo; la ruota, the wheel o fortune; the ruined tower; the wummin pope; the hangin man; il pazzo, the fool –

On the very word 'fool', DARNLEY, bottle in hand, appears, staggers.

– Zero. The King – nay, the knave, the knave o cups!

And CORBIE *shows us that very card.*

DARNLEY *is now supported by* BOTHWELL *and* BESSIE. *Drunk as he is,* DARNLEY *registers* RICCIO *with* MARY's *bare foot in his hands, on his lap.*

DARNLEY. What in hell's name is going on? Leave my wife alone – I'll bloody well –

DARNLEY *makes a drunken lunge.*

CORBIE. He will!

BOTHWELL. C'moan, man, wheest…!

BOTHWELL *bows low at* MARY*'s feet, acknowledges* RICCIO *perfunctorily.*

Madam, at your service. Seigneur Davy.

MARY. Bothwell, hoo daur you let him get intae sicc a state?

BOTHWELL. Madam… Ah nivir encouraged him. Ah… did advise him that mibbe he should caw canny. But he is the King.

MARY. He's only a laddie.

BOTHWELL *shrugs, ruffles* DARNLEY*'s drunken head indulgently.*

BOTHWELL. Ah ken, Ah ken… he hasna the heid for it yet.

DARNLEY. I'll tell you where I have been. I have been making friends among your nobles. On *your behalf.* You make no attempt to understand them or make them your allies. I'll tell you where I have been. On Tuesday, after the hunt, a great day's sport, we came upon a deserted little cove… near Aberdour. Very rocky… Bothwell and I swam a race across it. All the other nobles cheered. And I won. Didn't I, Hepburn…? I won!

MARY. Bothwell, I thocht I had askit ye for your help?

BOTHWELL. Madam, I hae missed ma ain dinner and ridden fifteen lang mile tae bring him safely harne, he isna ma responsibeelity…

MARY. Maister Hepburn, I am sorry.

Bessie, tak the Earl o Bothwell doon tae the kitchens directly and wake someone, middle o the nicht or no! Somethin hot for the Earl o Bothwell.

BESSIE *curtseys,* BOTHWELL *bows and both exit.* DARNLEY *lurches up to* MARY*, breathes in her face.*

DARNLEY. Ah Mary, Mary. I'm sorry… Give me a kiss.

She recoils.

Leave us alone, Seigneur Riccio!

MARY. Davy, stay exactly where you are!

RICCIO stays. Begins typing fast. DARNLEY crumples in humiliation. Slurring –

DARNLEY. Clack, clack, clack, like the tongues of foreigners… Italians. French… Only thing I can stand about the bloody French is the wine.

> (*Singing.*) Oh – oh – Give me twelve and twelve o the good claret wine,
> An twelve – and twel o the muskadine…

Mind you, the Scotch are as bloody bad. God made the Highlander out of a lump of dung… Then for the bloody Lowlander, He decided to economise on even that basic raw material.

What are you writing?

DARNLEY pulls the sheet out of the typewriter, crumples it up, throws it away.

Because it's too late at night. Go away, Seigneur Davy, I want to kiss my wife.

My lovely wife. My beautiful wife. D'you know she is the Queen? Therefore she must be beautiful.

She is though.

DARNLEY touches MARY's hair.

MARY. Davy, leave us.

RICCIO bows, goes – with palpable relief.

The royal couple are now alone. DARNLEY sobs like a child.

DARNLEY. Oh, Mary, Mary, I am sorry.

MARY. Aye, Henry, aye. You aye-weys are.

DARNLEY. Mary, Mary, I love you, hold me!

She rocks him and cradles him.

MARY. Wheesht, wheesht, Henry! Ssh.

CORBIE. Yin big bairn – and yin on the wey!

Scene Two

Rumplefyke

CORBIE. Haw – somethin hoat for the Earl o Bothwell!

BOTHWELL and BESSIE, dishevelled. He grabs her and kisses her lewdly.

BESSIE. Dinna!

She bites his mouth. He jumps apart from her.

BOTHWELL. Ya jaud ye, ye are as sherp as ye are soople.

BESSIE. Wheesht! The Queen'll hear us, or *somebody'll* –

BOTHWELL. The Queen! She's likely busy daen the same –

BOTHWELL kisses BESSIE, grabs at her up her skirt.

BESSIE. I dinna think sae!

BOTHWELL. Richt enough, he's ower fou tae even pish straight.

Ah wunner if he cin still pit a smile on her face?

BESSIE. Whiles. But no vera oaften.

BOTHWELL. Hoo dae ye ken?

BESSIE. Ah ken fine! What do you want to talk aboot the Queen for?

BOTHWELL. Ah dinna!

They kiss again, get right into it. When finally they break –

BESSIE. Bothwell, ma mistress kens naethin o the happiness you hae taught me.

BOTHWELL. Ah should hope no! The difference in oor ranks! Besides, I am a married man.

BESSIE. You ken fine whit I mean. I'm sure she has never kennt it for hersel.

BOTHWELL. Whit?

BESSIE. Love.

BOTHWELL. And her mairrit tae sicc a handsome long lad?

BESSIE. Ah'm sayin naethin!

BOTHWELL. And she doesna love him?

BESSIE. Mibbe aye… mibbe hooch aye!

BOTHWELL. Pair, pair Queen! Nae wunner her an Davy Riccio are sae thick thegither.

BESSIE. Noo dinna you start ony daft –

BOTHWELL. You're no tellin me it's true that the Queen and Davy Riccio –

BESSIE. Davy Riccio is as ugly as sin… He is a humphit backt wee puggy monkey o a man!

BOTHWELL *kisses* BESSIE *lewdly.*

BOTHWELL. Does he kiss her lik this? And does he stick his haun –

BESSIE. Dinna! You're makkin me shudder.

BOTHWELL. Maks a lot of women shudder, so I've heard. Maks them shiver when they see their smooth milk skin up agin greasy, creashy, warted skin, when they run their haun ower the bone-hard gnarl o the hump –

BESSIE. Dinna!

BOTHWELL. Oh aye! There is a big attraction – beauty wad fain keist wi ugliness, its opposite!

BESSIE. Naw –

BOTHWELL. Oh aye, oh aye, ma lassie. When you ken the weys o the warld as weel as this auld tod-fox o a man, here, does –

BESSIE. Does it no occur tae ye, maybe she looes Davy Riccio because he is the only man wha has ever touched her *withoot* he wants tae tummle her?

BOTHWELL. Och! Mibbe I should stap tummlin ye and ye'd looe me aw the better…?

BESSIE. Dinna!

She reaches for him.

BOTHWELL. Awricht, mibbe Ah'll no…

Touchin her, though! Ah hae heard it said a cat cin lukk at a queen, but never that a durty wee lowborn furriner can run his hauns aw ower her. Nae wunner the King droons his pair hornit heid in his cups, an the rumours…

BESSIE. He is a healer.

BOTHWELL. Och, Ah bet!

Pause.

What was aw yon wi the bare feet then? By God, the King was *bleezin*…

BESSIE. It's a healin airt! (*She holds out her own bare foot.*) Ilka bit o yer feet is… lik a map o the rest o yir body – oh, I dinnae ken, but yir ankle-banes are your briests…

BOTHWELL *sucks at her ankles.* BESSIE, *arches her back cups her own breasts and runs her hands down her body.*

…and the gimp-bit is your waist – an when you touch that bit on the fit it soothes that bit o the body…

Simultaneously BOTHWELL *was running his hand over her foot and finally tickles with his thumb between her toes.*

It works!

BOTHWELL. Ah'm trickery-Riccio... Ah'm Seigneur Davy... an you're the Queen... brawer than the Queen by faur...

BESSIE. I'm no!

BOTHWELL. Oh aye. An Ah'm Riccio! Touch ma hump. Gaun. It's hard and gnarlit, but it's got a bone in it. Go an.

It's lucky... a hunchback. Touch it! Touch. (*Whispers.*) Touch.

Scene Three

Rumours, Soughs and Chatters

The whole COMPANY *in a moving motif of whispers, passing letters, espionage.*

MARY *and* RICCIO *hard at work,* MARY *speaking French fast,* RICCIO *typing fast.*

A paper aeroplane swoops and loops across in front of them and lands. Silence. MARY *looks at it.* RICCIO *looks at it.* MARY *goes and picks it up.* RICCIO *tries to stop her, but she unfolds it and reads aloud –*

MARY. 'Seigneur Davy – beware o the bastard.'

Whit does this mean?

CORBIE. The bastard? That could be awmost hauf the court!

RICCIO takes it, screws it up into a ball and kicks it away in feigned scorn and bravado.

RICCIO. Parole! Parole!

CORBIE. Rumours, souchs and chatters in the court, an in the streets gowsters mairch vaunty an crawlin, chauntin oot hatred tae the Catholics.

Scene Four

Knox and Bothwell

Orange-Walk style, the COMPANY *approaching, sing out their hatred and bigotry with this, 'The Good and Godly Ballad'.*

ALL (*singing quietly, distant at first*).
Up wi the hunt. Up wi the hunt,
Tis noo the perfect day,
Jesus oor King is gane hunting,
Wha likes to speid they may.

(*Louder.*) Yin cursit fox lay hid in rocks,
This lang and mony yin day,
Devouring sheep whaur he micht creep,
Nane micht him fricht away.

(*Louder still.*) It did him guid to lap the bluid,
Of young and tender lambs,
Nane could he miss for all was his,
The young yins wi their dams.

(*Crescendo.*) That cruel beast, he never ceased,
By his usurpit power,
Under dispense to get oor pence,
Oor souls to devour.

(*Stamping, getting louder than ever.*) The hunter is Christ that hunts in haste!
The hounds are Peter and Paul,
The Pape is the fox, Rome is the rocks,
That rubs us on the gall.

KNOX *and* BOTHWELL *peel off from the rabble band.*

KNOX. I sympathise – as I am shair the Guid Lord does – wi the *zeal* which inspires destruction and indiscipline, although of course I condemn the act itsel.

And ye were saying…? Aboot the Queen…?

BOTHWELL. Och, I wis gey suspeecious o her tae, when she arrivit, and I hae much watcht for ony dissemblin I'd see there. And there is nane.

KNOX. You see nane?

BOTHWELL. Nane.

KNOX. Then beware o yir ain een, Bothwell. Beware of women, the charms o their hair. Beware, for adultery begins wi the eyes. Are ye mair virtuous than David? Are ye wiser than Solomon? Are ye stronger than Samson?

BOTHWELL. Ah am an ordinary man, but kinsman, I see… a wummin wha in six years in this country –

KNOX. – Has in her ain private chapel ilka Sunday heard the filthy Popish Mass.

BOTHWELL. Aye, in private. She has never heard Mass said in public. Ye ken how strang I am agin the Mass –

KNOX. Bothwell, it were mair fearfu tae me that yin Mass be heard in this realm than ten thousand men, armed and bristlin, were landed in a hundred foreign men o war upon oor shores.

BOTHWELL. And has she restored yin Scotch Catholic or yin abbey? Ye hae *dingit* doon the nests. The rooks *are* flown awa. Never tae return! Oh, the Queen does maintain her diplomatic contacts wi the Pope and aw Catholic Europe. Whit does it avail her? Jist words. 'Parole, Parole.'

There are three things they can send: Promises. Hard cash. Soldiers.

Hae they armed her? Hae they fattened oor skinny Scotch coffers? I say we maun maintain her safely on this throne – otherwise foreigners will be *forcit* to intervene to uphold the vera *idea* o sovereignty and legality.

On oor throne we hae a Catholic who has aye in word and deed affordit oor New Truth toleration.

And she is oor queen. Anointed by God.

KNOX. She says. And God says we are His, we belong to Him, justified by faith alone, and His election.

BOTHWELL. But I tell ye, Knox, there is a plan – you *ken* there is a plan – to bring doon the Queen and bring chaos to this realm.

KNOX. What wind have ye o this?

God – in His infinite mercy – aft-times does yase wicked men to punish other wicked men...

BOTHWELL. Maister Knox, stop hiding ahint your holiness just for once. I care naethin for Davy Riccio –

KNOX. Seigneur Davy is a poltroon and a vile knave.

BOTHWELL. Exactly. But I care *less* for him-that-ye-cry oor Bold Young King.

KNOX. He is a Protestant.

BOTHWELL. Is he? Oh aye, is that whit he is these days? Chynged his mind again, has he?

If aw his hums and haws were hams and haggises, the country wad be weel fed!

KNOX. – And he is the King.

BOTHWELL. The Queen's man.

KNOX. The King! And he kens he disna want to hae to rock Seigneur Davy's son in the royal cradle.

BOTHWELL. It is Henry's bairn she is big wi.

But wicked men – aye, Knox, ye dae ken wha they are and only ye can stap them – are yasin Henry Darnley's weakness as their strength.

KNOX. Hoo dae ye mak that oot?

BOTHWELL. I ask ye, the vera men wha rebelled agin the Queen when she mairrit Darnley, and wha were pit tae the horn and banisht tae Englan – they looe Darnley sae weel six months later that it is aw for advancement o him abune the Queen that they are plottin aw this mischief?

Acht! –

KNOX. I ken naethin o ony mischief.

BOTHWELL. Ye could forbid it, skail the hale thing fae the pulpit and stap it.

KNOX. I am a man o God. I care naethin for politics.

BOTHWELL. Because in this instance ye think the hail cowp will benefit ye and yir kirk.

KNOX. God's Kirk, Bothwell.

Plots and mischief? And whit benefit is there to you in stappin it? Keepin aw thing sweet for you and for her intae whase favour an influence ye hae ingratiated yoursel by crawling flattery?

BOTHWELL. I dinna think either queen nor maid ever accusit me o flattery.

KNOX. Oh aye, there is honey-flattery and there is sourrock-flattery. Such is the perverseness o women, I hear they like the sherp taste better.

BOTHWELL. As I love my kirk, and my country, so I love my queen. Nae mair.

Besides, the Crown cowps and the bliddy English will be up owerrinnin us again.

KNOX. Elizabeth is a Good Protestant...

BOTHWELL. I love the Scottish Crown.

KNOX. Oh aye. And what it will provide ye wi!

BOTHWELL. And ye wad suffer treason…?

KNOX. James Hepburn, Earl o Bothwell, kinsman, I tell you I am a man o God. My God has charged me, loud and plain, in the words o His ain Guid Book, no tae meddle wi the temporal filth o politiks. And it is my duty to obey my God. As God's kirk teaches its truth by the preachin o the word, then the spreadin o the word *demands* that all people be educated to read so that they may freely read and feed at his word, but there be nothin temporal or political in educating equally all God's subjects. If the kirk fight to feed them and claithe them it is only sae that they can maintain, on earth, God's *heavenly* kingdom.

If the word of God teaches men that all earthly palaces and power systems are robbers' caves then the punishment o wicked princes is the *duty* of their subjects.

I will leave it unto God to deal with the prince o this realm. I am shair the Good Lord will protect her, if she deserve to be protectit. Neither I, nor the yane true kirk have ony richt tae interfere. And I'd advise you no tae either, Maister Hepburn O'Bothwell.

Scene Five

Mummers and Murderers

Noise of drumbeat or clattering bones. Tumbling the first of a long string of them she has been setting up all during the last, a standing chain of dominoes, CORBIE announces flamboyantly as the last goes down –

CORBIE. Dominoes!

A now very pregnant MARY, *with* BESSIE *and* RICCIO *by her side, all very relaxed, domestic and easy, playing said game of dominoes. Couple of plays in silence, then –*

BESSIE. Ah'm chappin.

She does so. Picks up one.

MARY. Och, kickin!

BESSIE. They do say a boay kicks mair…

CORBIE. An that's juist on the inside, wait till he gets oot!

DARNLEY *bursts in looking weird, pale and strange. He is drunk.*

MARY. King Henry… so you jine us?

DARNLEY. And you aren't pleased to see me? It's me. Your husband. To while away the night with my sovereign, my wife, and my unborn son…

MARY. Of coorse we are pleased to see ye, Henry, maist gratified you have deserted mair congenial companions for our sake.

DARNLEY. …yes, with my sovereign, my wife, my unborn child and… assorted servants and menials, of course. Do excuse me, I did not *prostrate* myself before you all in greeting.

MARY. King Henry, you are drunk.

DARNLEY. Right you are, Queen Mary!

Not drunk. No. Just merry. And wishing to share my merriment with my poor lumpen wife.

I wonder if there can be a God, He arranges things so unfairly, eh? Deed it's true enough, you women get all the pain and burden, We Men, we get all the pleasure. Isn't that so, Seigneur Riccio?

MARY. Sit doon, Henry, if ye are going to drink a loving-cup with us.

DARNLEY. A loving-cup. I will indeed.

He drinks. Sound of music approaching.

BESSIE. Whit's that? Queen Mary, dinna let –

The rest of the COMPANY, *masked and strange, now disguised as* MUMMERS, *burst in;* MUMMERS 1, 2 *and* 3.

DARNLEY. Only a troop of travelling players. Here to entertain us.

CORBIE (*seeing trouble*). Mm-hm!

The MUMMERS *stand like stookies.*

DARNLEY. What are you going to perform for us tonight then?

CORBIE. Ah wonder...

They stand.

DARNLEY. Ha! Dumbshow... haha...!

Suddenly the MUMMERS *move.*

MUMMERS. Tara!

MUMMER 1 (*clears throat and announces*). The Mummers' *Masque of Salome!* –

MUMMER 2.
    A mellow-drama that entails
    Sex and lust at the court of King Herod –
    Plus the Dance of the Seven Veils!

A rude fart noise on a Harpo Marx horn.

CORBIE. Oh goody, the Bible! Ah love a story with a bit of blood and guts in it.

MUMMER 3 *pulls out a cushion with a very cardboard, or crudely improvised crown on it.* MUMMERS 1 *and* 2 *put exaggerated hands in the air and 'Ooh...!'*

MARY. Wha the hell are you?

DARNLEY. Just mumbling mummers, poor travelling players...

The MUMMERS *offer* DARNLEY *the crown.*

…Not at all! The crown does not fit me!

DARNLEY *places it with exaggerated ceremony on*
MARY*'s head.*

Tara! Hail the King!

MUMMER 2.

The King, he was called *Herod* –
He was King of all the Jews –
And he fell in love with his brother's wife –
Which was: Exceeding Bad News.

MUMMER 1.

Because a man called *John the Baptist* –

MUMMER 2.

Said: 'Herod! Upon my life,
It is written in the Law of the Prophets
Thou shalt not (*Parps horn.*) Bleep Thy Brother's Wife.'

MUMMER 1.

Herod looked at John the Baptist,
And his face turned deathly pale –

MUMMER 2.

Said: 'I'm the one that gives the bleeding orders',
And he clapped the poor prophet in gaol.

MUMMER 1.

Herod said –

MUMMER 2.

'A king can mairry wha he likes
Holy Joes like you can wheesht their din!'
And he promptly turned back to his feastin,
And got boozin and beastin in.

MUMMER 1.

To assuage his Foul Lust, nothing for it but he must
(*Bleep.*) The brother's wife in an adulterous lee-aison,

Then he done in the brother,
So they could marry one another –

MUMMER 2.

Acht! For murder, och! It's aye the silly see-aison!

MUMMER 1.

Noo the honeymoon's *been* for the *King* and *New Queen*,
And they are back to auld claes and parridge.
And the palace is the home y them and Salome –

MUMMER 2.

That's the new Queen's dochter by her first marriage.

DARNLEY *has been thrown a crude Salome-kit costume,
and he dons yashmak/falsies, etc. and begins lumbering
grossly and drunkenly.*

DARNLEY. Salome! That's *moi!*

MUMMER 1 *skelps him, he quietens down, suddenly
shocked to find himself their puppet.*

MUMMER 1.

Now, Herod was throwin a wee stag night,
For some visiting pot-entates.
Says the Queen –

MUMMER 2.

'Haw, ony chance… o Salome daen a wee dance
For the entertainment, like, o you and yir mates?'

And they lead out DARNLEY *as a gross Salome.*

MUMMER 1.

Now Salome had always been… big for her age,
Sortae… lamb dressed up as mutton.
Buxom and pretty wi a tassel on each titty,
And a jewel in her belly button.

And DARNLEY *as Salome begins to clumsily dance
sand-dance and mock striptease.*

So Salome done the seven veils
– At furst it wis jist fur a laugh –

She hooched, shimmied and skirled,
Shook, shoogled and birled,
Till they shouted, 'Get them aff!'

MUMMER 2.
Salome's mammy's look said, 'Go for it!'
So she didnae mess aboot –

MUMMER 1.
An soon – sweet sixteen wi slanty een –
She stood in her Birthday Suit.
Herod said –

And they force a bit of paper on MARY *– she's to read
Herod's part. More forcefully –*

Herod said – !

*And, all out of time, bullied and flustered, but trying to
pretend she's taking it as a joke –*

MARY.
'Och, Good Lord! Lassie, name your reward,
Ask for anything – yon wis great!'

DARNLEY (*as Salome, to* MARY *as Herod*).
'Give me the head of John the Baptist –
With some parsley, on a plate!'

And DARNLEY *points right at* RICCIO. *All three*
MUMMERS *rush at him, pull him to the ground, knives out
and he screams and clutches at* MARY'*s skirt.*

RICCIO. Justizia! Justizia! Sauvez ma vie! Justizia!

They stab him viciously and drag him off.

MARY, DARNLEY *and* BESSIE *are left. And* CORBIE.

MARY *glares her hatred at* DARNLEY, *who has crumbled
completely at the sight of the real and actual violence. When
he begins to sob,* MARY *runs at him.*

MARY. Kill me! Go on. Kill me tae. Kill me an your ain bairn.
Go an, ye micht as well. Plunge the knife in. Tear yin ain

bairn oot o ma tripes an strangle him wi yir ain hauns.
Because if you dinna he will grow up tae be revenged on ye.

Kill me. Kill me. Kill me!

MUMMER 1 *grabs* DARNLEY's *wrist very hard, holds it there.* MUMMER 2 *draws his sword against* DARNLEY's *throat.*

MUMMER 1. Naw, I wouldna dae that, young Henry…

MUMMER 2 (*tuts*). Regicide, that is.

MUMMER 1. Killing a king! Very nasty…

MUMMER 2. That's no hoo we dae things here in Scotland.

MUMMER 1. Never been heard of!

MUMMER 2. Not all through history…

MUMMER 1. *I've* never heard of it, have you, Jimmy?

MUMMER 2. Naw, Jock!

He sucks his teeth.

Not nice to kill a member of the fair sex either.

MUMMER 1. Not nice at the best of times but to kill wan that's thon wey wi a bairn…?

MUMMER 2. We couldnae hae it, Tam!

MUMMER 1. Neither we could, Wullie.

He hawks and spits. Bows.

Even though we are at your service, King Henry.

MUMMER 2. Behind you all the way, King Henry, we're your men, yes sir, oh aye!

MUMMER 1. Aren't we, Rab?

MUMMER 2. Aw the wey, Geordie.

DARNLEY. Is he dead?

MUMMERS *chuckle softly.*

MARY. Wha are ye? Wha are ye an wha did this?

CORBIE *goes circling and drumming herself up with this list and litany to a quiet frenzy.*

CORBIE.
There's Ruthven and Morton and Lindsay and Lethington,
Ormiston, Brunstane, Haughton and Lochlinnie,
There's Kerr o Fa'donside, Scott, and Yair and
    Elphinstone,
There's Ballantin and Douglas,
There's Ruthven and Morton...

She continues over the next, repeating this, becoming sotto voce.

MUMMER 1. King Henry, we need ye a wee minute, don't we, Jake?

MUMMER 2. We dae that, Eck. (*To* DARNLEY.) Ye see, sur... some o the townspeople are clamourin at the windaes –

MUMMER 1. There's been a wee bit o a disturbance an they're wonderin if the Queen's awricht.

They go, DARNLEY *flanked by* MUMMERS. MUMMER 1 *suddenly wheels back.*

(*At* MARY.) There's nae windaes in here, an Ah warn ye: there's ten big strang men staunin by that door wi the twa-handit sword and if ye try and get oot they will cut ye intae collops!

He exits. MARY, CORBIE, BESSIE, *alone and still. Silence.*

CORBIE. Blood!

MARY. He has killed oor maist special servant wha I looed richt well. I hate him.

CORBIE. Aye, hatred can be got in an instant, lik a bairn is, fattens faster in the wame an is, whiles, a lot langer in the nursin o it.

MARY (*to her unborn child*). So much are ye yir faither's bairn I fear for ye in the future.

CORBIE. A bairn's bairns are ill tae prosper!

Blood. Whit does that cry oot for?

MARY. Nae mair tears. I will think o a revenge. Bessie… Bessie, when they send ye for claes for me – I'm gonnae pretend ma labour has sterted, they'll hae to get me a midwife… we maun somehow get haud o ma black box wi Davy's foreign correspondence and somehow smuggle a message tae somebody…

Bothwell!

Tae onybody wha will help us!

Scene Six

Sweet Baby James, News for His Auntie Elizabeth, and a Gey Sore Sickbed for Darnley This Time

CORBIE *wheels on baby in a pram. She sings a sinister wee song, a familiar Scottish lullaby.*

CORBIE (*singing*).
Wee chookie burdie,
Tol-a-lol-a-lol,
Laid an egg on the windae sole,
The windae sole it began to crack,
And wee chookie burdie roared and grat.

CORBIE *wheels the pram.*

ELIZABETH *has a letter with a Polaroid snapshot of a baby in it.*

ELIZABETH. And so she has a son and heir.

They do say he is perfect. (*Looks at photo.*)

Well, 'James of Scotland', are you going to end up my heir
for want of a better or a nearer?

Surely not…

CORBIE *wheels the pram.*

CORBIE. Wee Jamie, eh? Born tae be King James the Saxt o
Scotland. Some day. If ye live sae lang… An awfy big name
for sicc a wee rid-faced scrawny shilpit wee scrap o
humanity, eh?

Dinna greet. Aye, wha's the lucky laddie tae have made it
this faur, eh? Eh?

ELIZABETH *with a hand mirror. She looks in it.*

ELIZABETH. A son and heir… and I am of but barren stock.
'The Virgin Queen.' Too old to whelp now at any rate.

CORBIE. Wheest, wheest, does your mammy love yir daddy,
eh? Eh? Does she no? Ach well, son, you'll no be the first
bairn i the warld conceivit in love and born intae hate.

DARNLEY *in his surgical mask lying on sickbed,* MARY
once again with that bowl of something, spoon-feeding him.

DARNLEY. Love me, Mary.

MARY. Sup this up, Henry…

DARNLEY. But you will love me again, Mary…? When I'm
better?

MARY. Aye, Henry… when you're better.

DARNLEY. Doctor said he didn't think it'd mark my face. You
don't think I'll be marked for ever? Surely smallpox doesn't
always –

MARY. Likely no, Henry.

DARNLEY. It's disgusting to you, isn't it? What if I'm all
pocked… Mary, could you ever let me back into your bed
again, with my face all –

MARY. It'll leave nae mark, Henry.

DARNLEY. Want to come back to your bed, be a proper husband again, Mary.

MARY. Eat. You're weak.

DARNLEY. Don't say that word. It's been a taunt at me ever since I was a boy.

MARY. You're still but a boy, Henry.

DARNLEY. And God help me but it's true! I'm weak. Wicked men used me, you were right, they would have killed me too. They used my weakness, my – Is loving you a weakness?

They made me jealous, I was a mad person, not myself, it wasn't...

Jealousy! It was a poison, it filled me up, they manipulated me, it wasn't my fault.

MARY. Wheesht. Eat.

DARNLEY. It was my fault.

MARY. Aye, but it wisna aw your faut, Henry. You're... only young yet, I tellt you.

DARNLEY. It's a long time ago now, Mary. I've changed. Honestly I'm not the same person! And our fine son is growing, eh?

MARY. Fat and bonny.

DARNLEY. I tell you, this last year... ever since that terrible night –

MARY *shrugs*.

MARY. We hae ither secretaries.

ELIZABETH *lets out an incoherent cry and crumples letter and photo*.

ELIZABETH. I do think it's hard to think of her so happy and me not! Dark deeds, bloody murders, plots against her life and throne, and she wins out again and again. All those involved just scatter when Darnley deserts them, most of the original rebels are pardoned and back in favour in Edinburgh, such is the wheel of fortune, and she is – if my spies tell me true – quite sweetly reconciled with the child-husband.

All her people love her, she has a husband and a fine healthy son.

Such is the wheel of fortune!... *'Oh, madam, you never wanted to marry!'* ...

How the hell do any of them know what I wanted?! Shut up! Shut up!

I don't know what I wanted.

She looks at herself in the mirror.

Lord! Grey hairs. Pluck them out!

CORBIE. Aye, King James the Saxt. Some day. And mair, mair than that, shall be. Some day. Wheesht. But watch ma lambie, watch!

Listen, once upon a time, aye, aye, oot on the open moor, caw, caw, an there was a moose thocht it was lord o the heather, and there was a foumart's den an it lay toom and empty. Sae the wee moose moved in and thocht it wis in heaven.

Till the foumart cam back an ett it fur its supper.

CORBIE *wheels the pram.*

DARNLEY *and* MARY *at his sickbed again.*

DARNLEY. We'll be happy again, you'll see.

MARY. Aye, Henry.

DARNLEY. And I can come to your bed again?

MARY. Once... once you're better o the smallpox, aye.

DARNLEY. I wish I could come back to the palace.

MARY. Soon.

DARNLEY. But you will stay here?

MARY. Aye. Downstairs. Richt ablow ye. I'm your wife.

DARNLEY. Will you come and sit with me tonight? We could
have music.

MARY. No, no the nicht, Henry. I hae tae gang tae a weddin –
ma best page is tae be merrit at the palace and I canny no go
to the feast o ma favourite, it widnae be lucky.

DARNLEY. Don't go.

MARY. I must. Fasten ma necklace, Henry.

*She bares the nape of her neck, hair forward and he fastens
clasp of her necklace and kisses her neck, burying his face in
her hair.*

DARNLEY. You smell beautiful. Amber, isn't it? I wish it could
drown out all the camphor of this sickroom, I wish, I wish –

MARY *bursts out suddenly –*

MARY. Henry, come with me to the wedding! Get up, Henry
Darnley! Quick! Now! Come and dance wi me!

DARNLEY. Mary, you know I'm sick, I can't go out of doors.

MARY. Of course you canna. Guidnicht, Henry.

DARNLEY. Kiss me?

*She does. Goes calmly from him. Straight to where
BOTHWELL is waiting for her. She goes into his arms. They
dance.*

MARY. To hell in a white petticoat wi you, Bothwell. Aye, I
will go. I maun go.

BOTHWELL. Ah only hud tae bide ma time…

They dance.

MARY. An thegither we shall *hae justice!*

MARY and BOTHWELL *kiss, sink together down to the floor, rolling over and over.*

Drums are building up to a crescendo. DARNLEY, *where* MARY *left him on his sickbed, stirs in his sleep, murmurs her name.*

DARNLEY. Mary…?

MARY. Justice!

An enormous explosion happens as, at Kirk o'Field, DARNLEY *and the house go up in flames.*

As smoke clears MARY *and* BOTHWELL *lie, still in each other's arms, on the floor. The rest of the* COMPANY *begin the accusatory chant. It builds.*

ALL. Burn the hoor! Burn the hoor! Burn the hoor!

And BOTHWELL *gets to his feet and runs off one way,* MARY *in another. The* COMPANY *go viciously, murderously after them. They are separated and exit on opposite sides.*

CORBIE, *alone among the clearing smoke, sings her devoid-of-pity, but nevertheless Lament for Lord Darnley in this, her version of the old ballad, 'The Twa Corbies'.*

CORBIE (*singing*).
 Twa weet black corbies in the snaw,
 Wi naethin in oor wames ataw,
 Tae the other yin Ah did say,
 'Whaur sall we gang and dine the day?'

 In ahint yon auld fail dyke,
 I ken there lies a new slain knight,
 And naebody kens,
 Naw, naebody kens,
 That he lies there,
 But his hawk and his hound and his lady fair.

 His hound is to the hunting gane,
 His hawk to fetch the wildfowl hame,

His lady has taen another mate,
And we may freely mak our dinner sweet.

Ye'll sit on his white hause-bane,
And I will pike oot his braw blue een,
And wi wan lock of his gowden hair,
We shall theek oor nest when it grows bare.

And ower his white banes when they are bare,
The wind shall blaw for ever mair.

The wind starts up, blowing around what snow and rose petals might still be strewn about the stage. CORBIE *can't speak, is no longer controlling things, or driving them forward; rather she is compelled to watch – and there's a sense of 'is compelled to watch all over again' – the last act of the tragedy.*

Scene Seven

Aw Thing Smashed and Skailt For Ever

ELIZABETH. Why me? Why? Why help her? Why does she come here, throwing herself on my mercy? Merciful God, I cannot *afford* to be merciful.

ADVISER 1. Kill her now.

ADVISER 2. It were a kindness.

ELIZABETH. I cannot welcome her here at court. I cannot help restore her to her throne in Scotland. I cannot be seen to condone rebellion against a rightful prince.

ADVISER 2. Exactly.

ADVISER 1. And you cannot keep her in prison indefinitely.

ELIZABETH. She is my honoured guest.

ADVISER 1. Yes, and some day she'll escape.

ADVISER 2. The focus of every Catholic hope, of every anti-Elizabeth faction in England.

ELIZABETH. Is she a witch?

ADVISERS 1 *and* 2. Ask the Scotch.

They fall back into the shadows, leaving her isolated and alone.

ELIZABETH. They split her from her Bothwell, drive him from their shores, they seize her infant son, strip her of her crown, lock her in a castle in the middle of an island and throw away the key.

And still she can charm some man into helping her escape.

God help me, why does she come to England when she could have sailed to bloody France!

ADVISERS *advance again, mill around* ELIZABETH –

ADVISER 2. Three years...

ADVISER 1. You really cannot keep her in prison indefinitely.

Seven... Eight...

ADVISER 2. – And some day she'll escape... thirteen, fift –

– and then fall back again into the shadows. With steely determination.

ELIZABETH. My subjects love me! I am the Virgin Queen! I love my good cousin Queen Mary and will continue to keep her my most honoured guest in all luxury in the lavish hospitality of my proudest castle. For her own safety.

And my so-called 'wise advisers' would have to trick me before I would consent to sign a warrant for her death.

Would have to trick me. Trick me. Trick me!

Her manic repetitions increase in volume, turn into obvious instructions. Thus summoned, ADVISERS *reappear by her side complete with a document. Without looking at it or*

them, she signs it. One of these absolutely impassive
ADVISERS *blots it, picks it up and blows on the signature.*

Careful! We do not want a blot!

The ADVISER *puts it inside his jacket. Both of them melt away.* ELIZABETH *stands alone, breathing, then exits in the other direction.*

A loud hammering. Noise gets louder and louder, stops.

MARY. Whit's that noise, Bessie?

BESSIE. It's nobbut the men, madam. It's jist thae bliddy men an their tools!

MARY. Is it ma scaffolding they are building? I ken it. Nineteen lang year…

Bessie, I am to die tomorrow.

BESSIE. Wheesht!

MARY. Last nicht I dreamed the strangest dream…

BESSIE. Wheesht!

MARY. I havena spared sae much as a thocht for him in years, yit… in my dream, large as life… larger! Bothwell.

BESSIE. Bothwell?

MARY. Aye. I ken… I ken… He's deid. A lang time deid. Mair nor a dizzen year. He dee'ed doublit up wud mad in a Danish jile. (*Long beat.*) You are greetan, Bess.

BESSIE. Greetin for us aw, madam.

MARY. Don't greet. I dinna.

I said: 'To Hell in a white petticoat wi you, Bothwell, oh aye, I will go. I maun go.'

Wis it love? No, no what you think, Jamie Hepburn, oh aye, ye were richt, I did – aye did… lust for ye. Wis that whit it wis? At the time I was ower innocent to ken whit wis steerin me? But I ken noo, Bothwell, I ken noo.

Dinna think it was lichtsomely or in love that I lay me doon wi ye, in the daurk. Naw, it wis in despair. Oh and wi a kind of black joy I reachit oot for ye to cover me and smother me and for yin moment snuff oot the hale birlin world in stillness. And ilka dawn I woke up wi ye, I saw disaster aw mapped oot for me, clear as my Davy's magic cairds. The ruined tower, the hangin man, the Empress on her Throne, Judgement...

And aw thing smashed and skailt for ever, tummeling aw aroon.

BESSIE. Madam, listen, wheesht, you maun...

MARY. – Call for ma confessor? Och, I ken what you are thinkin, Bessie!

BESSIE. Madam, dinna –

MARY. Your thinkan... that Ah'm thinkan...

MARY *shakes her head – 'Oh no, I'm not' – and manages the strangest wee laugh.*

Pair deid Darnley.

Violet velvet, Henry Darnley. Furs and pelts, baith civet and the genet. A press for you to keep your perfumes. A jewelled pomander. A bolt of cloth of gold, so much did I love you. Blue bonnets for your fools. Myself. That's what I gave you on oor wedding day.

And what did you ever give me, Henry Darnley?

A son. Wha will not lift a hand to save his mother. King of Scotland. Thus far. And even Auntie Elizabeth canna last for ever...

Poor Elizabeth. Tonight you dance in my dream. Tomorrow and ever after I will dance in yours.

Bessie, bind my een in silk! Ne criez point pour moi. J'ai promis pour vous!

One beat of absolute blackout and the terrible, final noise of the axeman's single heavy blow. Lights come back up and

CORBIE, *exhausted, devastated, has her hands over her ears and her eyes shut, blocking it out.*

Elsewhere, KNOX *is alone, on his knees with a scrubbing brush and a pail of soapy water. Scrubs harder and harder still at that indelible stain.*

CORBIE *opens her eyes. There is nothing more to say. She hears the noise of* KNOX*'s scrubbing, goes and looks at what he's doing. He doesn't see her or acknowledge her. Still silenced, she watches, bewildered, as all the rest of the* COMPANY, *except* MARY, *emerge transformed to seemingly bewitched and compelled brand-new-looking modern-day children, all now playing roles they have not chosen and scarcely seem to understand. As they come there could be weird slow playground bursts of leapfrog, peever, bools, fivestones. There are* WEE BETTY (ELIZABETH), WEE HENRY (DARNLEY), WEE RICHIE (RICCIO), *and* JAMES HEPBURN (BOTHWELL), *a playground bully, who runs up and kicks over* KNOX*'s bucket with a clang and a spill.* KNOX *gets up to his feet as if to challenge, but instead is transformed back to childhood too, into* SMELLY WEE KNOXXY, *who shrivels and whinges, puts up 'Keys' conceding, cringing, scared.* JAMES HEPBURN *pokes him viciously in the ribs then moves on laughing.* SMELLY WEE KNOXXY *rights the pail, then turns it upside down, then sits down on it, 'Oor Wullie style', making of himself an iconic Scottish picture of childhood. Once more he puts the 'Keys' up, he's not playing…*

CORBIE, *shocked from her silence and her fugue state by the noise of the spilt pail, watches, sorrowing, as the others set up in slow motion a game of skipping ropes.*

CORBIE.
> Bricht days, dull days, toom days, full days…
> Mair nor fower hunder years o Scotlan's historie –
> Aye, mair nor tongue can tell, sin that fell blow fell –
> Hae birled by, like the wind in the dark.
> An still we see Jock Tamson's bairns –
> Nobbut a wheen o loast weans in the park.

Scene Eight

Jock Tamson's Bairns

CORBIE *watches the slow-motion skipping ropes turn and, exasperated – as if 'Hell, if we've got to play this bloody game again, then let's get on with it' – calls out –*

CORBIE. Caw!

> *So they spring to full life, turn the ropes in real time, singing –*

GIRLS (*singing*).
>> Queen Mary, Queen Mary,
>> My age is *sixteen*.
>> My faither's a wino on *Glesca* green.
>> He's drank the Broo-money should dress me up braw.
>> Och, will nae bonny laddie come tak me awa?
>> *A! B! C! D! E!*

> MAREE (MARY) *appears, all by herself, very prominent, an outsider. She stands silent. Others nudge each other and look at her, hostile. Singing continues, tune changing to –*

>> On a mountain
>> Stands a lady.
>> Who she is I do not know.
>> All she wants is
>> Power and glory.
>> All she wants is a fine young man.

> WEE BETTY *wolf-whistles.*

WEE BETTY. Get her!

ANOTHER. Get swanky!

WEE BETTY. Big banana feet and legs long and lanky!

JAMES HEPBURN *wolf-whistles*.

JAMES HEPBURN. Hello, stranger!

WEE BETTY *and* ANOTHER *play a clapping game*.

> Hiya, stranger!
> I hope yir maw
> Thinks you're braw!
> Naw, naw,
> Nae chance! Nae danger!

WEE RICHIE. That's a sin. She's a wee orphan.

WEE BETTY. Little Orphan Annie! Show us your fanny.

ALL (*shocked*). Ow-ah!

> – *except* WEE BETTY *and* JAMES HEPBURN *who guffaw like the lewdest of children*.

WEE BETTY. What's your name anyway?

MAREE. Maree.

WEE BETTY. Maree?? Whit school do you go to?

JAMES HEPBURN. She means urr ye a left-fitter? Haw, stranger, d'you eat fish oan a Friday?

WEE BETTY. You a Tim?

JAMES HEPBURN. You a Fenian?

WEE BETTY. Are you a Pape?

MAREE. I'm a Catholic. Ih-hih.

WEE BETTY. Ih-hih? How you mean 'uh-huh'?

MAREE. Just…

She shrugs, trying not to rock the boat.

WEE BETTY. Well, away and get converted! Go an get born again. Away an jine the Bandy Hope, get tae the Tabernacle and go on a Crusade up the Tent Hall tin hut and get saved or somethin – Away and get saved for a sweetie!

They turn on SMELLY WEE KNOXXY. *They begin to torment him.*

WEE BETTY, JAMES HEPBURN, WEE HENRY *and* WEE RICHIE.
Wee Johnny Knox
Peed in the jawbox
When he thought his mammy wisnae lookin.
She hit it with a ladle
That was lying on the table,
Walloped him, and gied his heid a dooking!

SMELLY WEE KNOXXY (*singing*).
I'm H. A. P. P. Y.
I'm H. A. P. P. Y.
I know I am, I'm sure I am,
I'm H. A. P. P. Y.

I'm S. A. V. E. D.
I'm S. A. V. E. D.
I know I am, I'm sure I am,
I'm S. A. V. E. D.

JAMES HEPBURN. Haw! Get Smelly Wee Knoxxy!

Some grab SMELLY WEE KNOXXY, *some* MAREE.

WEE BETTY. Stick his heid up her skurt!

And they all shove SMELLY WEE KNOXXY*'s head up* MAREE*'s skirt, holding both of their struggling victims.* SMELLY WEE KNOXXY *is crying in real terror and distress.* MAREE *too.*

THE REST.
A queen cried Mary hud a canary
Up the leg o her drawers!

SMELLY WEE KNOXXY. Yuck it, youse! Yuck it. Dinnae! Ah doan't like lassies… Ma faither says I'm no tae play wi lassies!

WEE BETTY. Goan then! Get tae! Away an play wi yoursel then, stinky!

JAMES HEPBURN. Aye, git!

WEE BETTY. Skoosh!

RICHIE. Skeddaddle.

WEE BETTY. See you later, alligator!

She performs some sudden, physical, spiteful action on MAREE. *This is too much for* JAMES HEPBURN, *who's been, up to now, no slouch at being one of the torturers himself. He grabs* MAREE, *runs with her, crying out –*

JAMES HEPBURN. Leave the lassie alane!

All turn on the two of them, including SMELLY WEE KNOXXY, *who can see now how to taunt back.*

SMELLY WEE KNOXXY. Haw, Hepburn! Ah think you love her.

WEE BETTY. So do I, I think you love her! You gonny marry her?

JAMES HEPBURN. Nuh!

WEE BETTY. Aye, you urr! James Hepburn loves Maree Stewart!

THE REST. James Hepburn loves Maree Stewart! James Hepburn loves Maree Stewart!

JAMES HEPBURN. Ah jist says: (*Beat.*) Lea the Lassie Alane!

Freed, she looks right into his eyes. He into hers. She spits right in his face.

Right!

THE REST. Fight! Fight! Fight! Fight! Fight!

JAMES HEPBURN. I am the axeman.

THE REST. Kiss the axe.

SMELLY WEE KNOXXY. Pardon the executioner.

THE REST. And kiss the axe!

ALL.
>   Mary Queen of Scots got her head chopped off.
>   Mary Queen of Scots got her head chopped off!

WEE BETTY. And eftir you're deid, we'll share oot yir froacks
and pu aw the stones oot yir brooches and gie yir golden
slippers aw away to the Salvation Army, and we'll gie the
Saint Vincent de Paul –

JAMES HEPBURN. – Sweet fuck all!

WEE BETTY.
>   And eftir you're deid,
>   We'll pick up your heid,
>   Up aff the flair,
>   By the long rid hair –

JAMES HEPBURN. Wallop!

WEE HENRY. Haw-haw! It was just a wig! (*Beat*.) Yir heid
goes –

JAMES HEPBURN. Wallop!

And it stoats alang the flair like a great big... Tumshie!

ALL. Wallop! Bum... bum... bum... bum.

WEE HENRY. Skoosh!

ALL. SPLAT!!!

Pause.

WEE BETTY (*mock-tearful*).
>   And her wee dug...
>   Oh, her lovely wee dug...

Her lovely wee dug wi the big brown eyes that loved her
sooooo much...

Comes scooshing oot fae under her crimson skirts where it
has been hiding –

And skites aboot among the blood-rid *blood*, barking and
shiting itself!

Shriek of laughter from WEE BETTY, *totally wild and hysterical, scaring herself as much as it does* MAREE. *Silence.*

CORBIE *plays, with a marigold on its stalk, the old childhood game –*

CORBIE (*very quietly*).
Mary Queen of Scots got her head chopped off.
Mary Queen of Scots got her... head... chopped... off!

– And CORBIE *flicks the golden flower-head off.*

All the rest of the COMPANY *suddenly around* MAREE/MARY *and, at the word 'Off!', they grab up at her throat. And all freeze in a tableau.*

Blackout.

The End.